Praise for *Breaking the Bread*

"Never before has our Catholic Church had more resources or means to proclaim the Gospel or for us individually to live out our faith. Yet, with such an abundance of gifts we can sometimes feel overwhelmed in our efforts to absorb it all. *Breaking the Bread* instead chooses one 'pearl' among the many—the passages of Scripture entrusted to us each week in the cycle of lectionary readings—and unfolds and applies them using the *Catechism of the Catholic Church*. We should not be surprised that, thus saturated and shining with God's Word, this devotional manages to inspire and comfort, teach and clarify, call and concretize, all while preparing us to approach our Eucharistic King."

Most Reverend Thomas John Paprocki
Bishop of Springfield, Illinois

"In *Breaking the Bread*, Scott Hahn and Ken Ogorek have produced a readable, digestible, and thoroughly enjoyable work with reflections on the lectionary cycle for Year B. The work helps capture the spirituality of the liturgical year and the short questions at the end of each reflection invite the reader to deeper interior reflection and prayer. The work is not to be missed!"

Most Reverend Earl K. Fernandes
Bishop of Columbus, Ohio

"What a good idea: integrating the Sunday readings with excerpts from the *Catechism* and questions for prayer and personal reflection. With Dr. Hahn's customary profound and refreshing insight into Scripture and how it relates to us personally, this is a very useful resource."

Ralph Martin
President of Renewal Ministries
and Author of *A Church in Crisis*

"*Breaking the Bread* is an ideal resource for families who want to incorporate the Mass and Scripture mindfully into their practice of liturgical living in the home. Good for individual study for grownups or older kids, or perfect to use together as a family after Mass on Sundays and important feast days throughout the year, the brief but comprehensive reflections will help everyone better understand the readings we hear each week. What a blessing for all ages!"

Kendra Tierney
Mother of Ten and Author of *The Catholic All Year Compendium: Liturgical Living for Real Life*

"In this magnificent book, Scott Hahn and Ken Ogorek show through the lens of Mark's Gospel how God invites us into loving relationship with His Word. These rich and powerful reflections on the Sunday Mass readings help us to truly encounter, fall more deeply in love with, and give ourselves completely to Jesus. *Breaking the Bread* helps readers recapture a renewed sense of awe and wonder in listening to and appreciating the depth of God's word in their everyday lives."

Deacon Harold Burke-Sivers
Author of *Building a Civilization of Love: A Catholic Response to Racism*

"*Breaking the Bread* will be helpful not only for lay readers but especially for young priests trying to understand how to proclaim the combined message of the Sunday readings. Beautiful, well written, and easy to follow."

Marcus Grodi
Founder and President of the
Coming Home Network

"This book provides a beautiful way for Catholics to prepare for Sunday Mass. It offers a brief, expert guide to the lectionary texts for every Sunday of Year B through points of reflection presented with the help of beautiful graphics and great works of art. Our prayerful reflection is further enriched by texts from the *Catechism* that deepen our understanding of some aspect of the Scripture. With this prayer and study we can regularly engage the focus of the Sunday liturgy and allow it to enter our lives more deeply and fruitfully."

Lawrence Feingold
Professor of Theology, Kenrick-Glennon Seminary,
and Author of *Faith Comes from What Is Heard*

"This gorgeous book is a gem to be treasured. It masterfully brings each Sunday's Scripture alive with clarity and depth, revealing the wise design of the lectionary. A valuable resource for generations, this volume will offer fresh insight every time the Church contemplates these readings."

Elizabeth Foss
Founder of Take Up and Read

"Breaking the Bread provides an excellent template for praying with the Sunday Mass readings. Scott Hahn's exegesis gives us the context we need for understanding the Word of the Lord and Ken Ogorek's catechesis helps us apply it to our lives."

Matt Fradd
Host of Pints with Aquinas

BREAKING
the
BREAD

BREAKING
the
BREAD

A Biblical Devotional
for Catholics

Scott Hahn & Ken Ogorek

Year B

EMMAUS ROAD
PUBLISHING

Steubenville, Ohio
www.emmausroad.org

EMMAUS ROAD

Emmaus Road Publishing
1468 Parkview Circle
Steubenville, Ohio 43952

©2023 Scott Hahn and Ken Ogorek
All rights reserved. Published 2023
Printed in the United States of America

Library of Congress Control Number: 2023945648
ISBNs: 978-1-64585-348-0 hardcover | 978-1-64585-349-7 paperback
| 978-1-64585-350-3 ebook

Unless otherwise noted, Scripture quotations are taken from The Revised Standard Version Second Catholic Edition (Ignatius Edition) Copyright ©2006 by the Division of Christian Education of the National Council of the Churches of Christ in the United States of America. Used by permission. All rights reserved.

Excerpts from the *Lectionary for Mass for Use in the Dioceses of the United States of America, second typical edition* ©2001, 1998, 1997, 1986, 1970 Confraternity of Christian Doctrine, Inc., Washington, DC. Used with permission. All rights reserved. No portion of this text may be reproduced by any means without permission in writing from the copyright owner.

Excerpts from the Catechism of the Catholic Church, second edition, copyright ©2000, Libreria Editrice Vaticana—United States Conference of Catholic Bishops, Washington, DC. Noted as "CCC" in the text.

Cover design and layout by Allison Merrick

Liturgical Year B

Abbreviations ix
Introduction by Scott Hahn 1

Advent
First Sunday in Advent 6
Second Sunday in Advent 10
Third Sunday in Advent. 16
Fourth Sunday in Advent. 21

Christmas
Solemnity of the Blessed Virgin Mary,
   the Mother of God 28
Epiphany of the Lord 34
Baptism of the Lord 40

Ordinary Time
Second Sunday in Ordinary Time 46
Third Sunday in Ordinary Time. 52
Fourth Sunday in Ordinary Time. 56
Fifth Sunday in Ordinary Time 61
Sixth Sunday in Ordinary Time. 65
Seventh Sunday in Ordinary Time 71
Eighth Sunday in Ordinary Time 76

Lent
First Sunday of Lent 82
Second Sunday of Lent 88
Third Sunday of Lent 92

    Fourth Sunday of Lent 98

    Fifth Sunday of Lent. 103

    Palm Sunday of the Lord's Passion 109

EASTER

    Easter Sunday, the Resurrection of the Lord 116

    Sunday of Divine Mercy 122

    Third Sunday of Easter 127

    Fourth Sunday of Easter 133

    Fifth Sunday of Easter. 138

    Sixth Sunday of Easter. 142

    Seventh Sunday of Easter. 147

    Solemnity of the Ascension of the Lord. 152

    Pentecost. 159

ORDINARY TIME

    Solemnity of the Holy Trinity 164

    Solemnity of the Most Holy Body
       and Blood of Christ 170

    Ninth Sunday in Ordinary Time 175

    Tenth Sunday in Ordinary Time 179

    Eleventh Sunday in Ordinary Time 184

    Twelfth Sunday in Ordinary Time 189

    Thirteenth Sunday in Ordinary Time 194

    Fourteenth Sunday in Ordinary Time 198

    Fifteenth Sunday in Ordinary Time 204

    Sixteenth Sunday in Ordinary Time 209

    Seventeenth Sunday in Ordinary Time 214

Eighteenth Sunday in Ordinary Time 218

Transfiguration of the Lord 223

Nineteenth Sunday in Ordinary Time 228

Twentieth Sunday in Ordinary Time. 232

Twenty-First Sunday in Ordinary Time 238

Twenty-Second Sunday in Ordinary Time 242

Twenty-Third Sunday in Ordinary Time 246

Twenty-Fourth Sunday in Ordinary Time 252

Twenty-Fifth Sunday in Ordinary Time. 256

Twenty-Sixth Sunday in Ordinary Time 262

Twenty-Seventh Sunday in Ordinary Time. 266

Twenty-Eighth Sunday in Ordinary Time 271

Twenty-Ninth Sunday in Ordinary Time 276

Thirtieth Sunday in Ordinary Time 281

Thirty-First Sunday in Ordinary Time. 286

Thirty-Second Sunday in Ordinary Time 291

Thirty-Third Sunday in Ordinary Time 295

Solemnity of Our Lord Jesus Christ,
   King of the Universe 300

INDEX OF IMAGES 305

Abbreviations

Ad Trall.	St. Ignatius of Antioch, *Epistle to the Trallians*
Adv. haeres.	St. Irenaeus, *Adversus Haereses* (Against Heresies)
Adv. Marc.	Tertullian, *Adversus Marcionem* (Against Marcion)
AG	Second Vatican Council, *Ad Gentes* (Decree on the Mission Activity of the Church)
Apol.	Tertullian, *Apologeticum* (Apology for the Christians)
can.	cannon
CIC	*Codex Iuris Canonici* (Code of Cannon Law)
De fide orth.	St. John Damascene, *De fide orthodoxa* (An Exposition of the Orthodox Faith)
De inc.	St. Athanasius, *De Incarnatione* (On the Incarnation)
De unit.	St. Cyprian, *De Unitate Ecclesiae* (On the Unity of the Catholic Church)
DV	Second Vatican Council, *Dei Verbum* (Dogmatic Constitution on Divine Revelation
Faust	St. Augustine, *Contra Faustum* (Against Faustus)
GS	Second Vatican Council, *Gaudium et Spes* (Pastoral Constitution on the Church in the Modern World)

Hom. in Ex.	Origen, *Homilies on Exodus*
LG	Second Vatican Council, *Lumen Gentium* (Dogmatic Constitution on the Church)
Opusc.	St. Thomas Aquinas, *Opscula* (Treatises)
PG	J. P. Migne, ed., Patrologiae Cursus Completus: Series Graeca
PL	J. P. Migne, ed., Patrologiae Cursus Completus: Series Latina
RMiss	John Paul II, *Redemptoris Missio* (Encyclical Letter on the Permanent Validity of the Church's Missionary Mandate)
SC	Second Vatican Council, *Sacrosanctum Concilium* (Constitution on the Sacred Liturgy)
Serm.	Augustine, *Sermones* (Sermons)
UR	Second Vatican Council, *Unitatis Redintegratio* (Decree on Ecumenism)

Introduction

What the great rabbi Samson Raphael Hirsch said of his coreligionists is just as true of mine. The catechism of the Jew, he said, is the calendar. It is in the prescribed readings for synagogue and home that God's chosen people learn about his works and ways. It is through the individual feast days that they learn the stories—and the overarching story—of salvation history.

Thus, every year unfolds as a succession of lessons not only in history but in personal and collective identity. We remember the marvels the Lord has done, and we remember who we are in relation to Him. This is the way of biblical religion. It is the way of all our ancestors in the Catholic faith. It is the way every generation has passed God's Revelation to their children and grandchildren.

In the modern era, we've recovered an ancient Greek term to describe the process. We call it "catechesis." But the process itself has developed down the centuries. For millennia, our ancestors had no access to books—and most of them could not read. There were no printing presses or other media available. The word "catechesis" literally meant "instruction by word of mouth," and indeed, the word most people heard was *viva voce*.

Today we have a superabundance of media. We can use online audio and video—and even books!—to learn the truths of doctrine and the facts of sacred history. And yet, the primary way we hand on and receive the Revelation of God is still by word of mouth.

It is liturgical. The Church proclaims the Word every day from the ambo and preaches it from the pulpit. The lectionary provides the ordered sequence of readings that ensures the consistency and fullness of the message.

And never has the lectionary been so rich. Through all of history—in all the Church—the lectionary was designed to be delivered over the course of a single year. But the revised lectionary, introduced in 1969, covered three years. That made possible the inclusion of far more Scripture from more parts of the Bible.

The old lectionary's Sunday readings had been chosen almost exclusively from the Gospels and Epistles. The new lectionary, by contrast, employed much of the content of most of the books of the Bible, both the Old and New Testaments. In the old lectionary, the Sunday Gospels had not been selected in any representative or proportionate way; there were, I believe, only four readings from Mark in a year, and the parable of the Prodigal Son was not read at all. In the new scheme, Mark gets every congregation's attention for a full year, and the Prodigal Son has become a familiar figure.

Within a year of the publication of the revised lectionary, the Presbyterian churches adapted it for their own use, and Anglican and Lutheran bodies soon adapted it as well. Now, for the first time since the Protestant Reformation, perhaps the majority of Christians in the world are hearing the same Scriptures read on any given Sunday.

The other great development in catechesis in my lifetime has been the Catechism of the Catholic Church. Like the revised lectionary, it includes far more Scripture than any of its predecessors. With these two documents in hand, we are better equipped than ever to transmit the faith to our families, our neighbors, our parishioners, our friends. We have been baptized for this task.

This book coordinates the weekly lectionary texts with relevant selections from the Catechism, as well as points for reflection and suggestions for further reading. It has been my pleasure to collaborate on this project with my friend Kenneth Ogorek, a man who has quietly done more than anyone I know for the renewal of catechesis in the United States.

In these pages, calendar and catechism come together with Holy Writ in a way that is new—and I hope will be effective in an unprecedented way.

On the day of His Resurrection, Jesus walked with two disciples from Jerusalem to the village of Emmaus. It was the immediate aftermath of the great festival of the Jewish year, a pilgrim feast that drew all Hebrew males to the Holy City; yet, the disciples were sad and confused. Then Jesus "interpreted to them in all the Scriptures the things concerning himself." He began "with Moses and all the prophets" and continued through the other books (see Luke 24:27). Afterward, the disciples' hearts were burning with joy and an eagerness to spread the word. Later that day, Jesus encountered the Apostles and told them about his fulfillment of "everything written about [Him] in the law of Moses and the prophets and the psalms" (Luke 24:44).

Our current moment brings us back to that great moment in the history of catechesis. The revised lectionary and the comprehensively biblical Catechism make possible the kind of instruction Jesus Himself gave on that first Easter Sunday. So may we share the faith we have received, and so may our hearers respond with burning hearts and zeal for evangelization.

Scott Hahn

Advent

Year B

First Sunday in Advent

ISAIAH 63:16B–17, 19B; 64:2–7

PSALM 80:2–3, 15–16, 18–19

1 CORINTHIANS 1:3–9

MARK 13:33–37

Watch for Him

The new Church year begins with a plea for God's visitation. "Oh that you would rend the heavens and come down," the prophet Isaiah cries in today's First Reading.

In today's Psalm, too, we hear the anguished voice of Israel, imploring God to look down from His heavenly throne—to save and shepherd His people.

Today's readings are relatively brief. Their language and message are deceptively simple. But we should take note of the serious mood and penitential aspect of the liturgy today as the people of Israel recognize their sinfulness, their failures to keep God's covenant, their inability to save themselves.

But God is faithful, Paul reminds us in today's Epistle. He is Our Father. He has hearkened to the cry of His children, coming down from heaven for Israel's sake and for ours to redeem us from our exile from God, to restore us to His love.

In Jesus, we have seen the Father (see John 14:8–9). The Father has let His face shine upon us. He is the Good Shepherd come to guide us to the heavenly kingdom (see John 10:11–15). No matter how far we have strayed, He will give us new life if we turn to Him, if we call upon His holy name, if we pledge anew never again to withdraw from Him.

In this Advent season, we should see our own lives in the experience of Israel. As we examine our consciences, can't we, too, find that we often harden our hearts, refuse His rule, wander from His ways, withhold our love from Him? As Paul says today, He has given us every spiritual gift—especially the

Eucharist and penance—to strengthen us as we await Christ's final coming. He will keep us firm to the end—if we let Him.

So, in this season of repentance, we should heed the warning—repeated three times by Our Lord in today's Gospel—to be watchful, for we know not the hour when the Lord of the house will return.

When the time comes, your body and soul will separate temporarily. (Unless, that is, Jesus comes again in glory before you experience physical death.) At any rate, when the Lord of the house comes, your body will have incorruptible life. Be alert, so that your everlasting life will be pleasant.

> By death the soul is separated from the body, but in the resurrection God will give incorruptible life to our body, transformed by reunion with our soul. Just as Christ is risen and lives for ever, so all of us will rise at the last day. (CCC 1016)

Sometimes we know in advance that we're going to meet the Lord. Even if death isn't imminent, a serious sickness or even advanced age makes a person well suited to celebrate the Sacrament of Anointing of the Sick. Knowing that the time is coming can be a blessing.

The proper time for receiving this holy anointing has certainly arrived when the believer begins to be in danger of death because of illness or old age. (CCC 1528)

SHOW US, LORD, YOUR LOVE; AND GRANT US YOUR SALVATION.

PSALM 85:8

What are some ways I can treat my body that show I expect it to be with me forever?

What aged person might I visit in the near future?

Jesus, as Advent begins, help me to be watchful. Help me prepare to celebrate Your birth. Make me aware of Your presence in my life. Bless me with readiness for Your return in glory. Amen.

Second Sunday in Advent

ISAIAH 40:1–5, 9–11

PSALM 85:9–10, 11–12, 13–14

2 PETER 3:8–14

MARK 1:1–8

Straighten the Path

Our God is coming. The time of exile—the long separation of humankind from God due to sin—is about to end. This is the Good News proclaimed in today's liturgy.

Isaiah in today's First Reading promises Israel's future release and return from captivity and exile. But as today's Gospel shows, Israel's historic deliverance was meant to herald an even greater saving act by God—the coming of Jesus to set Israel and all nations free from bondage to sin, to gather them up and carry them back to God.

God sent an angel before Israel to lead them in their exodus toward the promised land (see Exodus 23:20). And He promised to send a messenger of the covenant, Elijah, to purify the people and turn their hearts to the Father before the day of the Lord (see Malachi 3:1, 23–24). John the Baptist quotes these, as well as Isaiah's prophecy, to show that all of Israel's history looks forward to the Revelation of Jesus. In Jesus, God has filled in the valley that divided sinful humanity from Himself. He has reached down from heaven and made His glory to dwell on earth, as we sing in today's Psalm.

He has done all this not for humanity in the abstract but for each of us. The long history of salvation has led us to this Eucharist, in which our God comes again and our salvation is near. And each of us must hear in today's readings a personal call. Here is your God, Isaiah says. He has been patient with you, Peter tells us in today's Epistle.

Like Jerusalem's inhabitants in the Gospel, we have to go out to Him, repenting our sins, renouncing all the self-indulgence that makes our lives a spiritual wasteland. We have to straighten out our lives so that everything we do leads us to Him. Today let us hear the beginning of the Gospel and again commit ourselves to lives of holiness and devotion.

John's baptism certainly had significance. Yet, he acknowledged that another Baptism was coming, one mightier than his. Christian Baptism brings with it several awe-inspiring effects.

> The fruit of Baptism, or baptismal grace, is a rich reality that includes forgiveness of original sin and all personal sins, birth into the new life by which man becomes an adoptive son of the Father, a member of Christ and a temple of the Holy Spirit. By this very fact the person baptized is incorporated into the Church, the Body of Christ, and made a sharer in the priesthood of Christ. (CCC 1279)

Those whom John baptized apparently had functioning consciences. They acknowledged their sins. We have an obligation to form our conscience well so that if we sin we will know it, and ideally we will make judgments that will help us avoid wrongdoing.

A well-formed conscience is upright and truthful. It formulates its judgments according to reason, in conformity with the true good willed by the wisdom of the Creator. Everyone must avail himself of the means to form his conscience. (CCC 1798)

What are the means of forming my conscience? How do I avail myself of them?

How well and how often do I defer to others when it's appropriate, acknowledging that "one mightier than I is coming"?

Heavenly Father, I thank You for drawing so close to me, during this Advent season and always. Help me, by Your grace and mercy, to persevere in devotion to you as well as the life of holiness that is Your will for me. Amen.

PREPARE THE WAY *of* THE LORD,

MAKE STRAIGHT HIS PATHS:

ALL FLESH SHALL SEE

THE SALVATION OF GOD.

LUKE 3:4, 6

BLESSED IS HE

WHO COMES IN THE

NAME *of* THE LORD!

BLESSED IS THE KINGDOM

OF OUR FATHER DAVID

THAT IS TO COME!

MARK 11:9, 10

sanctification of his name, the coming of the kingdom, and the fulfillment of his will. The four others present our wants to him: they ask that our lives be nourished, healed of sin, and made victorious in the struggle of good over evil. (CCC 2857)

Do I pray the Lord's Prayer daily? Do I pray it slowly enough to focus on its beautiful words?

In the Lord's Prayer we refer to *Our* Father, not just *my* Father. How does this affect my perception of the various communities around me?

Lord Jesus Christ, King of the Universe, I place my life in Your loving hands. I adore and worship You as my Master and Teacher. May I always hear, listen to, and act on Your voice, until You return in glory. Amen.

we have been loved by Him, freed by His blood, and transformed into "a kingdom, priests for his God and Father" (Revelation 16; see also Exodus 19:6; 1 Peter 2:9). As a priestly people, we share in His sacrifice and in His witness to God's everlasting covenant. We belong to His truth and listen to His voice, waiting for Him to come again amid the clouds.

Truth is so important that Jesus associates it with the basic reason for His Incarnation. Because of truth's importance, we must take it very seriously. We must belong to the truth, listening for the voice of Our Lord.

> False oaths call on God to be witness to a lie. Perjury is a grave offence against the Lord who is always faithful to his promises. (CCC 2163)

"Thy kingdom come." Each time we pray the Our Father we acknowledge God's lordship and pledge our allegiance to the one kingdom that is truly under Him. This truth in fact sets us free to pursue the priorities of God's kingdom—and in the process have a profoundly positive impact on the world around us.

> In the Our Father, the object of the first three petitions is the glory of the Father: the

A Royal Truth

What's the truth Jesus comes to bear witness to in this last Gospel of the Church's year?

It's the truth that in Jesus God keeps the promise He made to David of an everlasting kingdom, of an heir who would be His Son, "the first born, highest of the kings of the earth" (see 2 Samuel 7:12–16; Psalm 89:27–38).

Today's Second Reading, taken from the Book of Revelation, quotes these promises and celebrates Jesus as "the faithful witness." The reading hearkens back to Isaiah's prophecy that the Messiah would "witness to the peoples" that God is renewing His "everlasting covenant" with David (see Isaiah 55:3–5).

But as Jesus tells Pilate, there's far more going on here than the restoration of a temporal monarchy. In the Revelation reading, Jesus calls Himself "the Alpha and the Omega," the first and last letters of the Greek alphabet. He's applying to Himself a description that God uses to describe Himself in the Old Testament: the first and the last, the One who calls forth all generations (see Isaiah 41:4; 44:6; 48:12).

"He has made the world," today's Psalm cries, and His dominion is over all creation (see also John 1:3; Colossians 1:16–17). In the vision of Daniel we hear in today's First Reading, He comes on "the clouds of heaven"—another sign of His divinity—to be given "glory and kingship" forever over all nations and peoples.

Christ is King. His kingdom, while not of this world, exists in this world in the Church. We are a royal people. We know

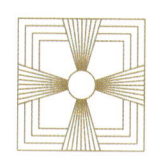

Solemnity of Our Lord Jesus Christ, King of the Universe

DANIEL 7:13–14

PSALM 93:1, 1–2, 5

REVELATION 1:5–8

JOHN 18:33B–37

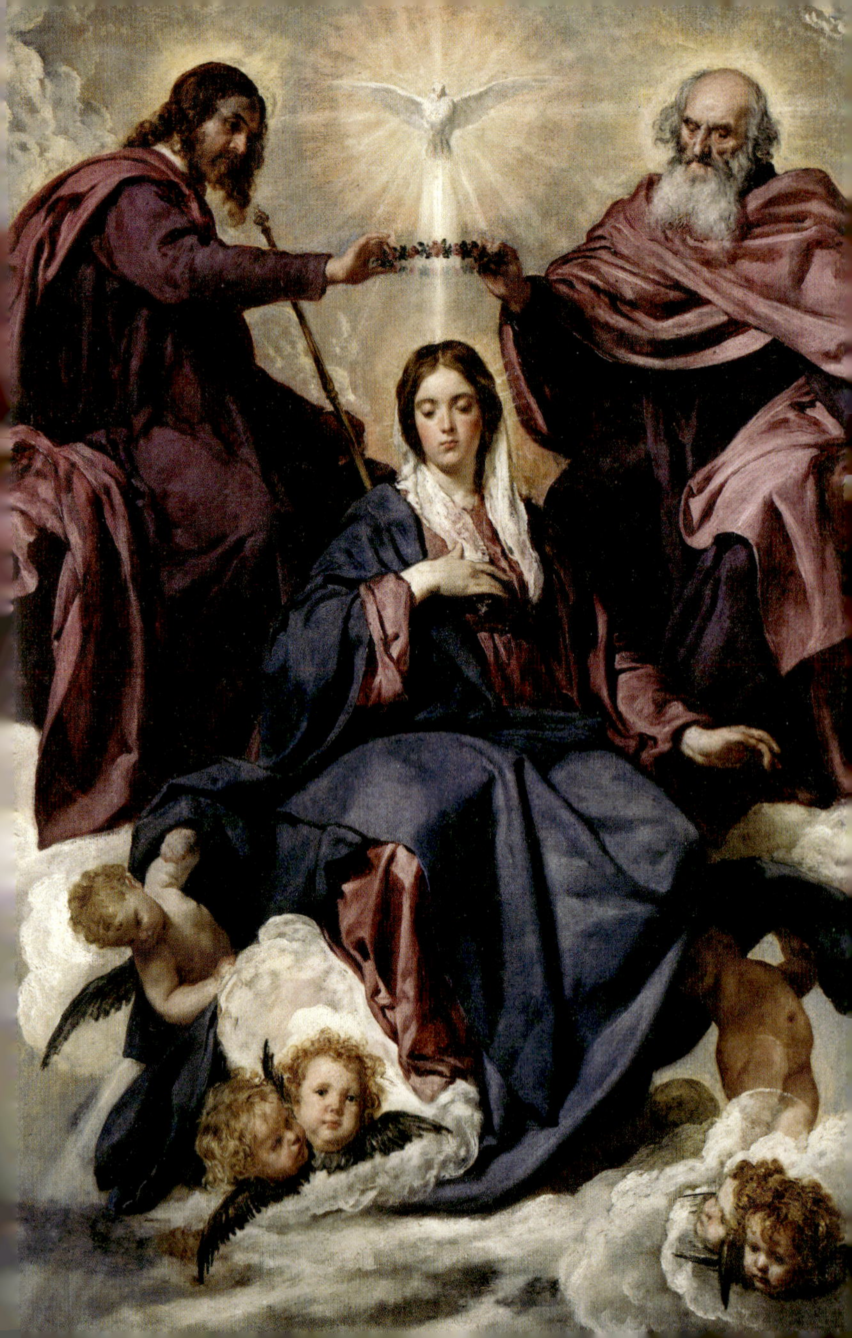

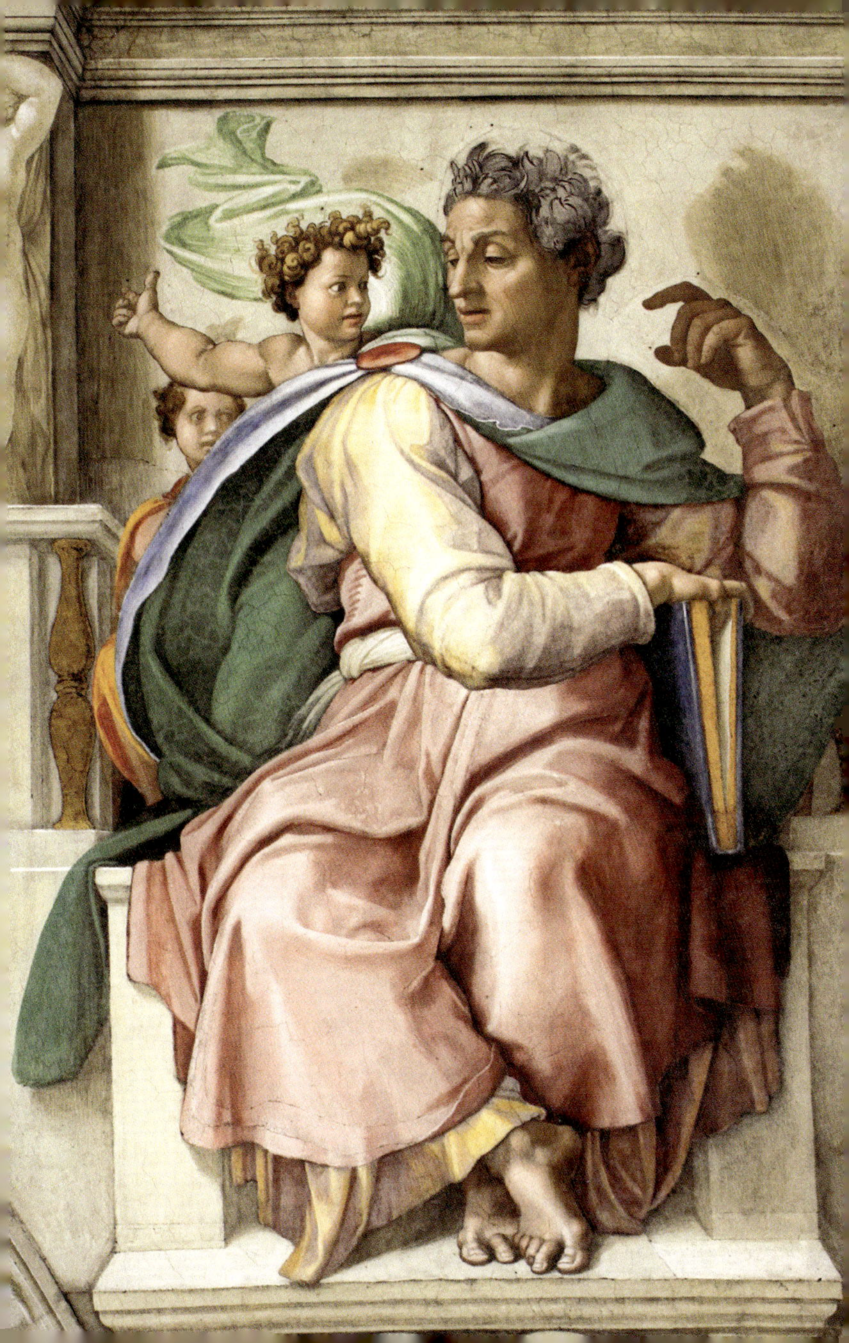

Third Sunday in Advent

ISAIAH 61:1–2A, 10–11

LUKE 1:46–48, 49–50, 53–54

1 THESSALONIANS 5:16–24

JOHN 1:6–8, 19–28

One Who Is Coming

The mysterious figure of John the Baptist, introduced in last week's readings, comes into sharper focus today. Who he is, we see in today's Gospel, is best understood by who he isn't.

He is not Elijah returned from the heavens (see 2 Kings 2:11), although like Elijah, John dresses in the prophet's attire (see Mark 1:6; 2 Kings 1:8) and preaches repentance and judgment (see 1 Kings 18:21; 2 Chronicles 21:12–15). While he is not Elijah in the flesh, John is nonetheless sent in the spirit and power of Elijah to fulfill his mission (see Luke 1:17; Malachi 3:23–24).

Neither is John the prophet that Moses foretold, although he is a kinsman and speaks God's Word (see Deuteronomy 18:15–19; John 6:14). Nor is John the Messiah, though he has been anointed by the Spirit since he was in the womb (see Luke 1:15, 44).

John prepares the way for the Lord (see Isaiah 40:3). His baptism is symbolic, not sacramental. It is a sign given to stir our hearts to repentance. John shows us the One upon whom the Spirit remains (see John 1:32), the One who fulfills the promise we hear in today's First Reading (see Luke 4:16–21). Jesus' bath of rebirth and the Spirit opens a fountain that purifies Israel and gives to all a new heart and a new Spirit (see Zechariah 13:1–3; Ezekiel 36:24–27; Mark 1:8; Titus 3:5).

John comes to us in the Advent readings to show us the light, that we might believe in the One who comes at Christmas. As we sing in today's Responsorial, the Mighty

One has come to lift each of us up, to fill our hunger with bread from heaven (see John 6:33, 49–51).

And as Paul exhorts in today's Epistle, we should rejoice, give thanks, and pray without ceasing that God will make us perfectly holy in spirit, soul, and body—that we may be blameless when Our Lord comes.

We need Baptism in the first place because without it we can't live the holiness to which God calls us; we can't attain the degree of justice that He intends. Ever since the first sin of the first human person, all of creation waited breathlessly for the light to come into our world, dispelling sin's darkness forever.

> By his sin Adam, as the first man, lost the original holiness and justice he had received from God, not only for himself but for all human beings. (CCC 416)

Jesus is the Word of God. God speaks His Word to us in various ways, especially through Scripture and Church teaching. Reflecting on God's Word—and acting upon it—helps to keep us on a good path.

The Word of God is a light for our path. We must assimilate it in faith and prayer and put it into practice. This is how moral conscience is formed. (CCC 1802)

THE SPIRIT OF THE LORD IS UPON ME, BECAUSE HE HAS ANOINTED ME TO BRING GLAD TIDINGS TO THE POOR.

ISAIAH 61:1

How does original sin influence me?

What are some ways I might put the Word of God into practice in my community this week?

Holy Spirit, make Your presence known in my life as You have throughout salvation history. Help me, Spirit of God, to see that Jesus truly is the light of the world. Amen.

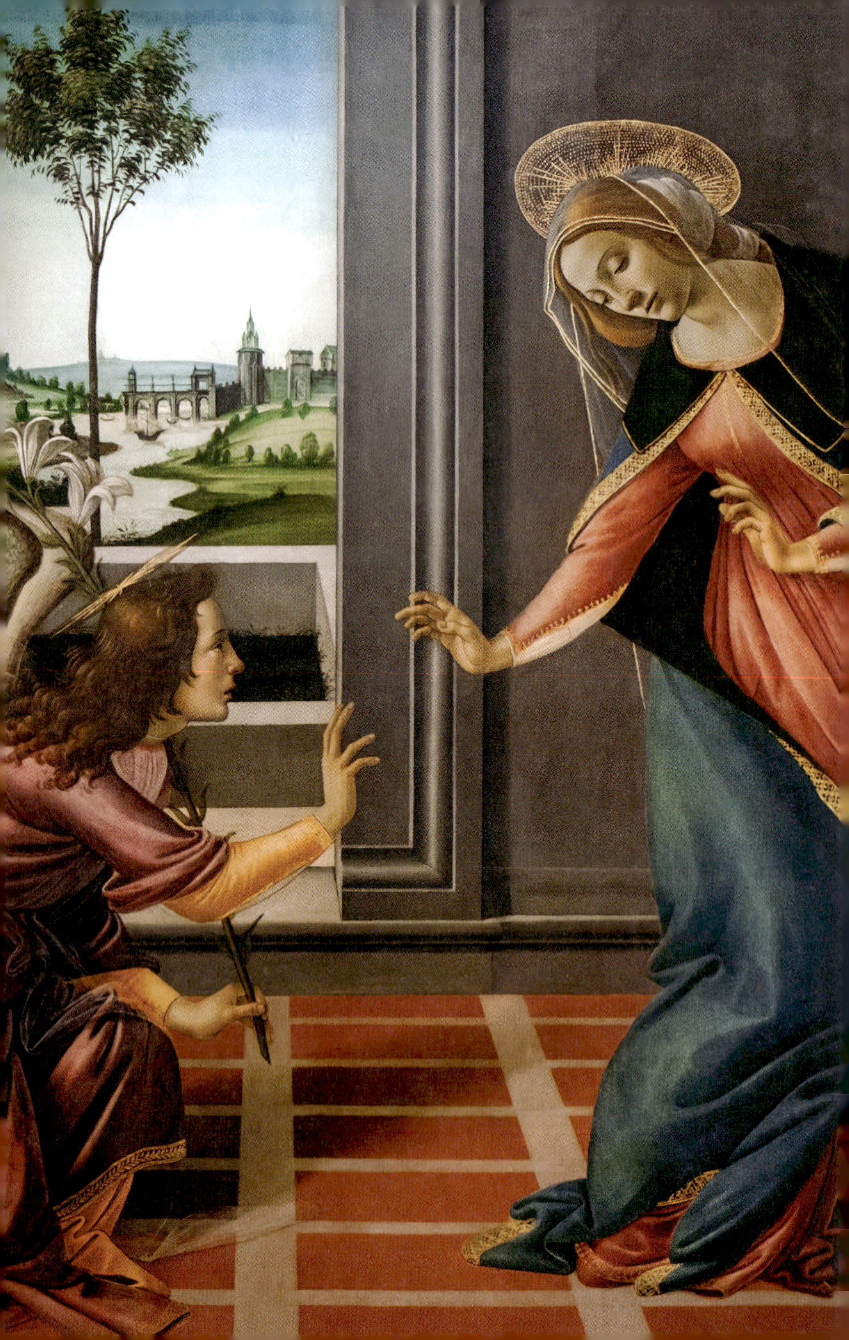

Fourth Sunday in Advent

2 SAMUEL 7:1–5, 8B–12, 14A, 16

PSALM 89:2–3, 4–5, 27, 29

ROMANS 16:25–27

LUKE 1:26–38

The Mystery Kept Secret

What is announced to Mary in today's Gospel is the revelation of all that the prophets had spoken. It is, as Paul declares in today's Epistle, the mystery kept secret since before the foundation of the world (see Ephesians 1:9; 3:3–9).

Mary is the virgin prophesied to bear a son of the house of David (see Isaiah 7:13–14). Nearly every word the angel speaks to her today evokes and echoes the long history of salvation recorded in the Bible.

Mary is hailed as the daughter Jerusalem, called to rejoice that her king, the Lord God, has come into her midst as a mighty Savior (see Zephaniah 3:14–17).

The One whom Mary is to bear will be Son of "the Most High"—an ancient divine title first used to describe the God of the priest-king Melchizedek, who brought out bread and wine to bless Abraham at the dawn of salvation history (see Genesis 14:18–19).

Jesus will fulfill the covenant God makes with His chosen one, David, in today's First Reading. As we sing in today's Psalm, He will reign forever as the highest of the kings of the earth, and He will call God "my father." As Daniel saw the Most High grant everlasting dominion to the Son of Man, Christ's kingdom will have no end (see Daniel 4:14; 7:14).

He is to rule over "the house of Jacob"—the title God used in making His covenant with Israel at Sinai and again in promising that all nations would worship the God of Jacob (see Exodus 19:3–6 and Isaiah 2:1–5).

Jesus has been made known, Paul says, to bring all nations to the obedience of faith. We are called with Mary today to marvel at all that the Lord has done throughout the ages for our salvation. And we, too, must respond to this annunciation with humble obedience: that His will be done, that our lives be lived according to His Word.

Everything we believe about Mary essentially relates to our faith in her Son. As we hope one day to be filled with grace according to the potential for holiness that God gives us, so Mary lived her whole life. Sinless, she conceived, bore, and raised the One who conquers sin forever.

> From among the descendants of Eve, God chose the Virgin Mary to be the mother of his Son. "Full of grace," Mary is "the most excellent fruit of redemption" (SC 103): from the first instant of her conception, she was totally preserved from the stain of original sin and she remained pure from all personal sin throughout her life. (CCC 508)

Mary's parents no doubt taught her to pray by word and example. Mary, in turn, together with St. Joseph, provided Jesus with an excellent model of closeness to the Father through prayer. It is in this way that the life of prayer passes from one generation to the next: those taught to pray in turn teach others by example and word.

> The Christian family is the first place for education in prayer. (CCC 2694)

How often do I pray the Hail Mary? How might I do so more often if need be?

How is prayer taught and modeled in my family?

Most Blessed Virgin Mary, you desire all of God's people to know your Son, Jesus, as their Savior, God, and King. Please pray that as I prepare to celebrate the newborn King's birth, I will enthrone Him as the Lord of my life. Amen.

BEHOLD, I AM

THE HANDMAID

of THE LORD.

MAY IT BE DONE TO ME

ACCORDING TO

YOUR WORD.

LUKE 1:38

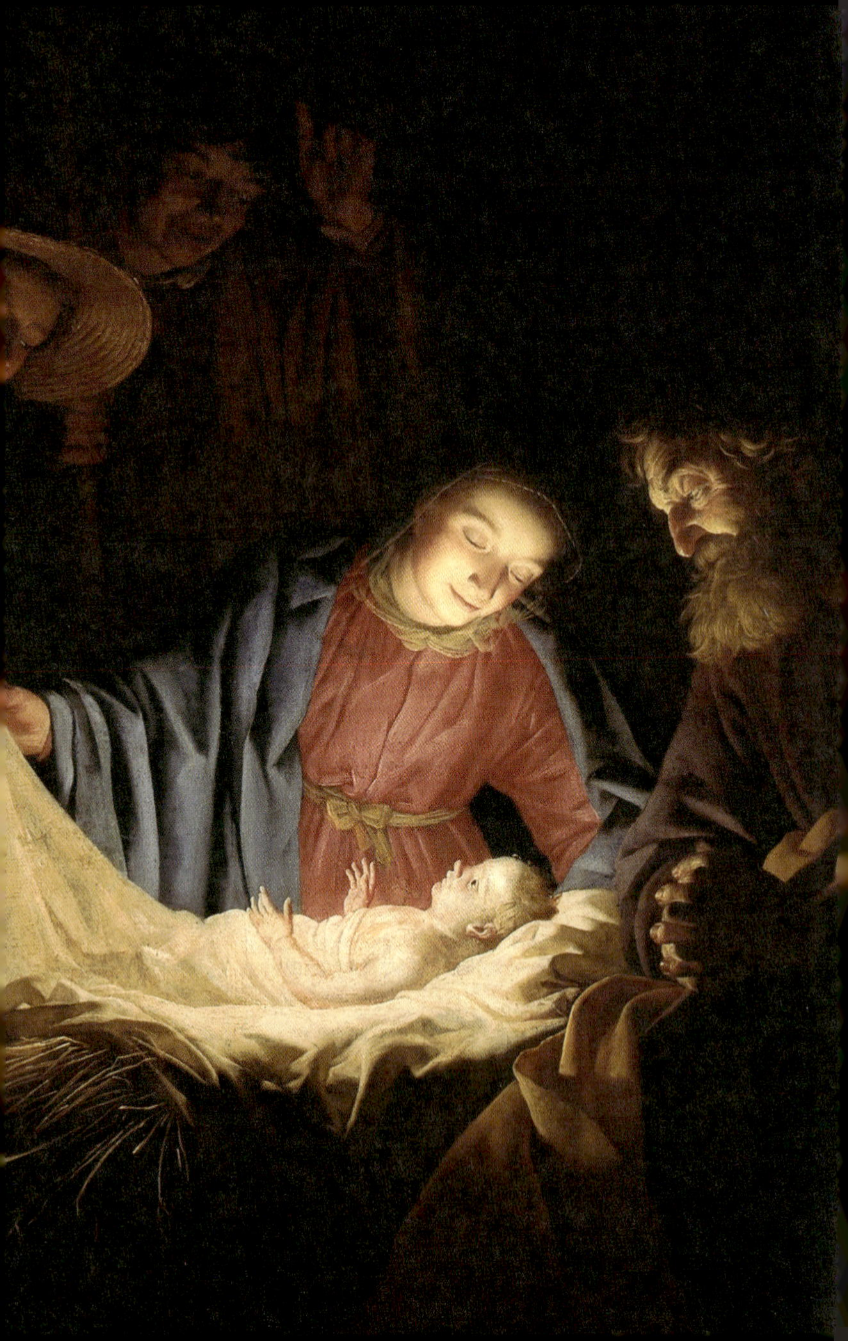

Christmas

Year B

Solemnity of the Blessed Virgin Mary, the Mother of God

NUMBERS 6:22–27

PSALM 67:2–3, 5, 6, 8

GALATIANS 4:4–7

LUKE 2:16–21

Children of God

Today we give thanks to Mary, the Mother of God. Her response to the angel, born of a humble heart, brought us life and salvation through the child conceived in her womb.

From before all ages, God had destined her for this decisive role in salvation history. She was to be the woman who, in the fullness of time, would bear God's only Son, as Paul tells us in today's Epistle.

In times past, God spoke to His chosen people, the Israelites, through prophets (see Hebrews 1:1–2), and imparted His blessings upon them through His priests, as we hear in today's First Reading. But now, He has sent His Son to reveal His glory and His kingdom, to make His way of salvation known to all nations, as we sing in today's Psalm. In the infant lying in the manger, God has shone His face upon us (see John 14:8–9).

Jesus is made a child of Israel, an heir of God's covenant with Abraham, by His circumcision in today's Gospel (see Genesis 17:1–14). And we have been made adopted sons and daughters by Baptism, which is the circumcision of Christ, the true circumcision (see Colossians 2:11; Philippians 3:3).

As children of God, Paul says today, we are heirs of the Father's blessings, which He promised to bestow on all peoples through the descendants of Abraham (see Genesis 12:3; 22:18; Galatians 3:14). This is the blessing Aaron imparted to the nation of Israel, the people descended from Abraham. And this blessing comes to us through Mary and her child.

This is the Good News of great joy that the shepherds make known in Bethlehem today (see Luke 2:10). Like the shepherds, we should make haste today to find Jesus with Mary and Joseph and to glorify God for His blessings. And like Mary, we should keep His Word and reflect upon it, letting it dwell richly in our hearts (see Colossians 3:16).

Mary heard God's call to reflect in her heart often throughout her earthly life. She in turn reached out to God so as to encounter Him in prayerful reflection. Each of us is called by God—today and every day—to converse in a prayerful relationship with our loving Creator.

> God tirelessly calls each person to this mysterious encounter with Himself. Prayer unfolds throughout the whole history of salvation as a reciprocal call between God and man. (CCC 2591)

The shepherds made an amazing message known to anyone who would listen. It's as if these shepherds were on a mission—because they were! The solemnity we celebrate today reminds us of a special grace of the Holy Spirit. This grace helps us pursue, among other good goals, that of bearing witness to the Christian faith, strengthened in a unique and powerful way when we are Confirmed.

> Confirmation perfects Baptismal grace; it is the sacrament which gives the Holy Spirit in order to root us more deeply in the divine filiation, incorporate us more firmly into Christ, strengthen our bond with the Church, associate us more closely with her mission, and help us bear witness to the Christian faith in words accompanied by deeds. (CCC 1316)

Mary was open to new life. Had she not been eager to collaborate with God—even if His intentions for her life differed from what she'd envisioned—where would we be today? Although Mary's motherhood came about in an entirely unique way, the Solemnity of the Blessed Virgin Mary, the Mother of God, includes a message for each of us: Let us be open to new life and encourage this beautiful openness among spouses.

> The regulation of births represents one of the aspects of responsible fatherhood and motherhood. Legitimate intentions on the part of the spouses do not justify recourse to morally unacceptable means (for example, direct sterilization or contraception). (CCC 2399)

Reflect on Mary's response to the angel Gabriel's message. How do I respond when something great is asked of me?

Do I understand the Church's teaching on human sexuality? Are there aspects that I need to study further?

Most Holy Trinity—Father, Son, and Holy Spirit—as each of You has a special relationship with our Blessed Mother, please help my devotion to Mary deepen and my reliance on the Blessed Virgin as my prayerful intercessor strengthen throughout my earthly life, until I enter the joy of heaven with You. Amen.

IN THE PAST GOD SPOKE

TO OUR ANCESTORS

THROUGH *the* PROPHETS;

IN THESE LAST DAYS,

HE HAS SPOKEN TO US

THROUGH THE SON.

HEBREWS 1:1–2

Epiphany of the Lord

ISAIAH 60:1–6

PSALM 72:1–2, 7–8, 10–11, 12–13

EPHESIANS 3:2–3A, 5–6

MATTHEW 2:1–12

Newborn King

Today the child born on Christmas is revealed to be the long-awaited king of the Jews. As the priests and scribes interpret the prophecies in today's Gospel, he is the ruler expected from the line of King David, whose greatness is to reach to the ends of the earth (see Micah 5:1–3; 2 Samuel 5:2).

Jesus is found with His mother, just as David's son, Solomon, was enthroned alongside his Queen Mother (see 1 Kings 2:19). And the magi come to pay Him tribute, as once kings and queens came to Solomon (see 1 Kings 10:2, 25).

Jesus' coming evokes promises that extend back to Israel's beginnings. Centuries before, an evil king seeking to destroy Moses and the Israelites had summoned Balaam, who came from the East with two servants. But Balaam refused to curse Israel. Instead, he prophesied that a star and royal staff would arise out of Israel and be exalted above all the nations (see Numbers 22:21; 23:7; 24:7, 17).

This is the star the three magi follow. And like Balaam, they refuse to be tangled in an evil king's scheme. Their pilgrimage is a sign that the prophesies in today's First Reading and Psalm are being fulfilled. They come from afar, guided by God's light, bearing the wealth of nations, to praise Israel's God.

We celebrate today our own entrance into the family of God and the fulfillment of God's plan that all nations be united with Israel as coheirs to His Fatherly blessings, as Paul reveals in today's Epistle.

We, too, must be guided by the root of David, the bright morning star and the light of the world (see Revelation 22:16;

Isaiah 42:6; John 8:12). As the magi adored Him in the manger, let us renew our vow to serve Him, placing our gifts—our intentions and talents—on the altar in this Eucharist. We must offer to Him our very lives in thanksgiving. No lesser gift will suffice for this newborn King.

Even as a baby, Jesus has a universal appeal. The magi are drawn to Him. The Church, Christ's Mystical Body, includes a universality—a catholicity—in her mission.

> "Having been divinely sent to the nations that she might be 'the universal sacrament of salvation,' the Church, in obedience to the command of her founder and because it is demanded by her own essential universality, strives to preach the Gospel to all men": "Go therefore and make disciples of all nations, baptizing them in the name of the Father and of the Son and of the Holy Spirit, teaching them to observe all that I have commanded you; and Lo, I am with you always, until the close of the age." (CCC 849, quoting Vatican II, *Ad Gentes*, no. 1; and Matthew 28:19–20)

EPIPHANY OF THE LORD • 37

The magi were overjoyed when they knew they were on the verge of paying homage to Jesus. Their journey no doubt felt complete upon attaining their goal. Knowingly or not, these travelers experienced happiness due to their closeness to God-with-us.

> Man is made to live in communion with God in whom he finds happiness: "When I am completely united to you, there will be no more sorrow or trials; entirely full of you, my life will be complete" (St. Augustine, *Conf. 10*, 28, 39: PL 32, 795). (CCC 45)

What is my joy level as I approach the weekly opportunity to do Jesus homage—to worship and adore him at Mass?

How might I capture the joy of the magi at this opportunity?

St. Joseph, you witnessed remarkable events, always trusting that God in His righteousness was making His holy will manifest. Pray for me that, like the magi, I may adore Jesus, especially when I kneel before Him in the Eucharist. Amen

WE SAW HIS STAR

AT HIS RISING

and HAVE COME

TO DO HIM HOMAGE.

MATTHEW 2:2

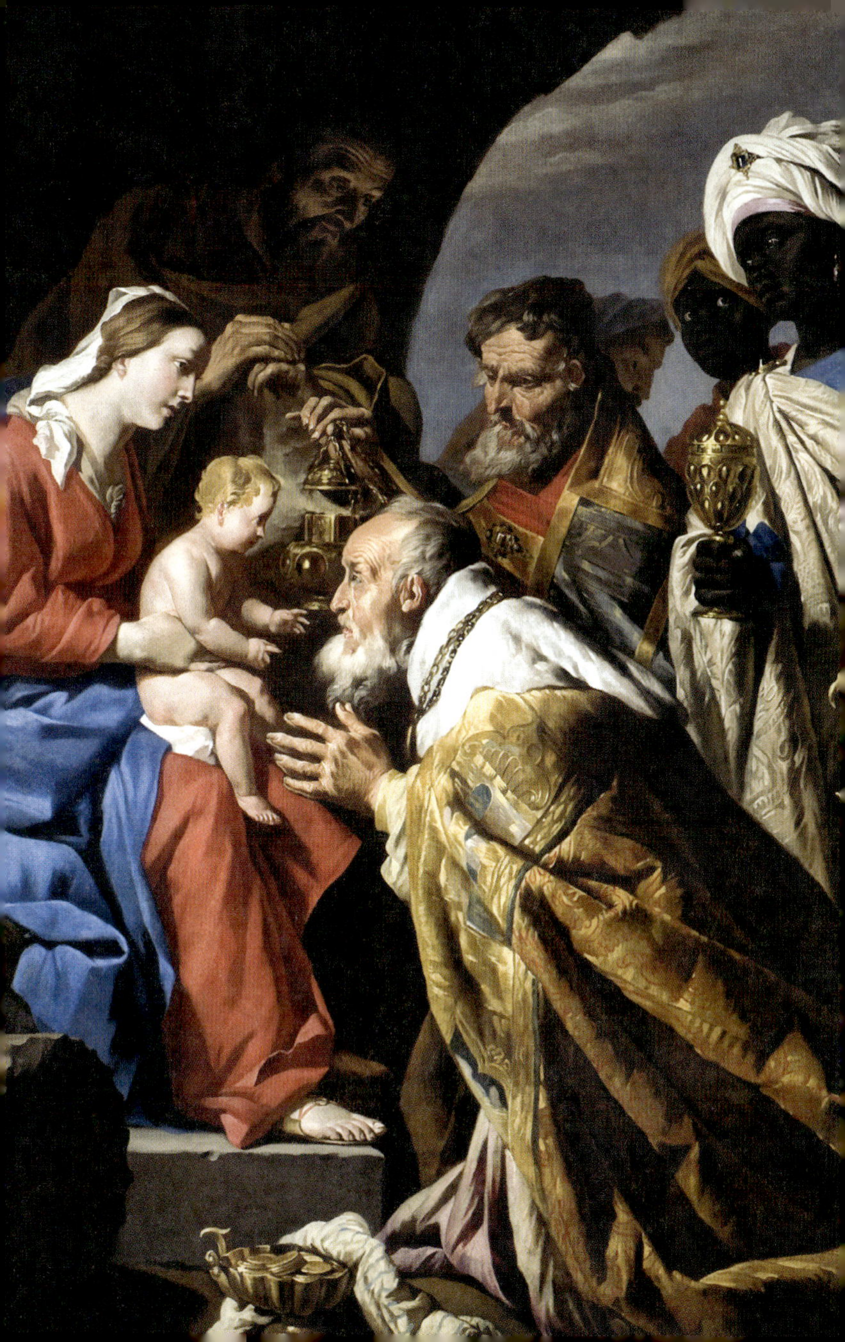

Baptism of the Lord

ISAIAH 42:1–4, 6–7 (OR 55:1–11)

PS 29:1–2, 3–4, 3, 9–10 (OR ISAIAH 12:2–3, 4BCD, 5–6)

ACTS 10:34–38 (OR 1 JOHN 5:1–9)

MARK 1:7–11

The Anointing

The liturgy last week revealed the mystery of God's plan: that in Jesus, all peoples, symbolized by the magi, have been made "coheirs" to the blessings promised to Israel. This week, we're shown how we claim our inheritance.

Jesus doesn't submit to John's baptism as a sinner in need of purification. He humbles Himself to pass through Jordan's waters in order to lead a new "exodus"—opening up the promised land of heaven so that all peoples can hear the words pronounced over Jesus today, words once reserved only for Israel and its king, that each of us is a beloved son or daughter of God (see Genesis 22:2; Exodus 4:22; Psalm 2:7).

Jesus is the chosen servant Isaiah prophesies in today's First Reading, anointed with the Spirit to make things right and just on earth. God puts His Spirit upon Jesus to make Him "a covenant of the people," the liberator of the captives, the light to the nations. Jesus, today's Second Reading tells us, is the one long expected in Israel, "anointed . . . with the Holy Spirit and power."

The word "Messiah" means "one anointed" with God's Spirit. King David was "the anointed of the God of Jacob" (see 2 Samuel 23:1–17; Psalm 18:51; 132:10, 17). The prophets taught Israel to await a royal offshoot of David, upon whom the Spirit would rest (see Isaiah 11:1–2; Daniel 9:25). That's why the people of the whole Judean countryside and all the inhabitants of Jerusalem were going out to John.

But it isn't John they're looking for. God confirms with His own voice what the angel had told Mary: Jesus is the Son of the Most High, come to claim the throne of David forever (see Luke 1:32–33).

In the Baptism that He brings, the voice of God will hover over the waters as fiery flame, as we sing in today's Psalm. He has sanctified the waters, making them a passageway to healing and freedom—a fountain of new birth and everlasting life.

The Spirit is present when God acknowledges Jesus as His beloved Son. This same Holy Spirit helps us, too, to acknowledge the Lord God and all He has revealed to us. The gift of faith is one that Our Father is pleased to offer.

> Faith is a supernatural gift from God. In order to believe, man needs the interior helps of the Holy Spirit. (CCC 179)

Exactly why Jesus submitted to John's baptism we don't know for sure. Certainly, Jesus had no reason to seek forgiveness of sins. Christian Baptism, though, is very much focused on forgiveness. The cleansing waters of Baptism link us to Jesus and pour out upon us the Holy Spirit, the Third Person of the Blessed Trinity.

Baptism is the first and chief sacrament of the forgiveness of sins: it unites us to Christ, who died and rose, and gives us the Holy Spirit. (CCC 985)

JOHN SAW JESUS APPROACHING HIM, AND SAID: BEHOLD THE LAMB OF GOD WHO TAKES AWAY THE SIN OF THE WORLD.

CF. JOHN 1:29

How often do I pray for the gift of faith? How might I ask the Holy Spirit more consistently to help strengthen my belief?

God offers words of affirmation to Jesus here. Who in my community needs my affirmation, and how soon will I give it?

St. John the Baptist, you encouraged others to focus on Jesus, showing the humility proper to one who recognizes the Messiah. Pray for me, that I may humbly accept Jesus' boundless love for me. Amen.

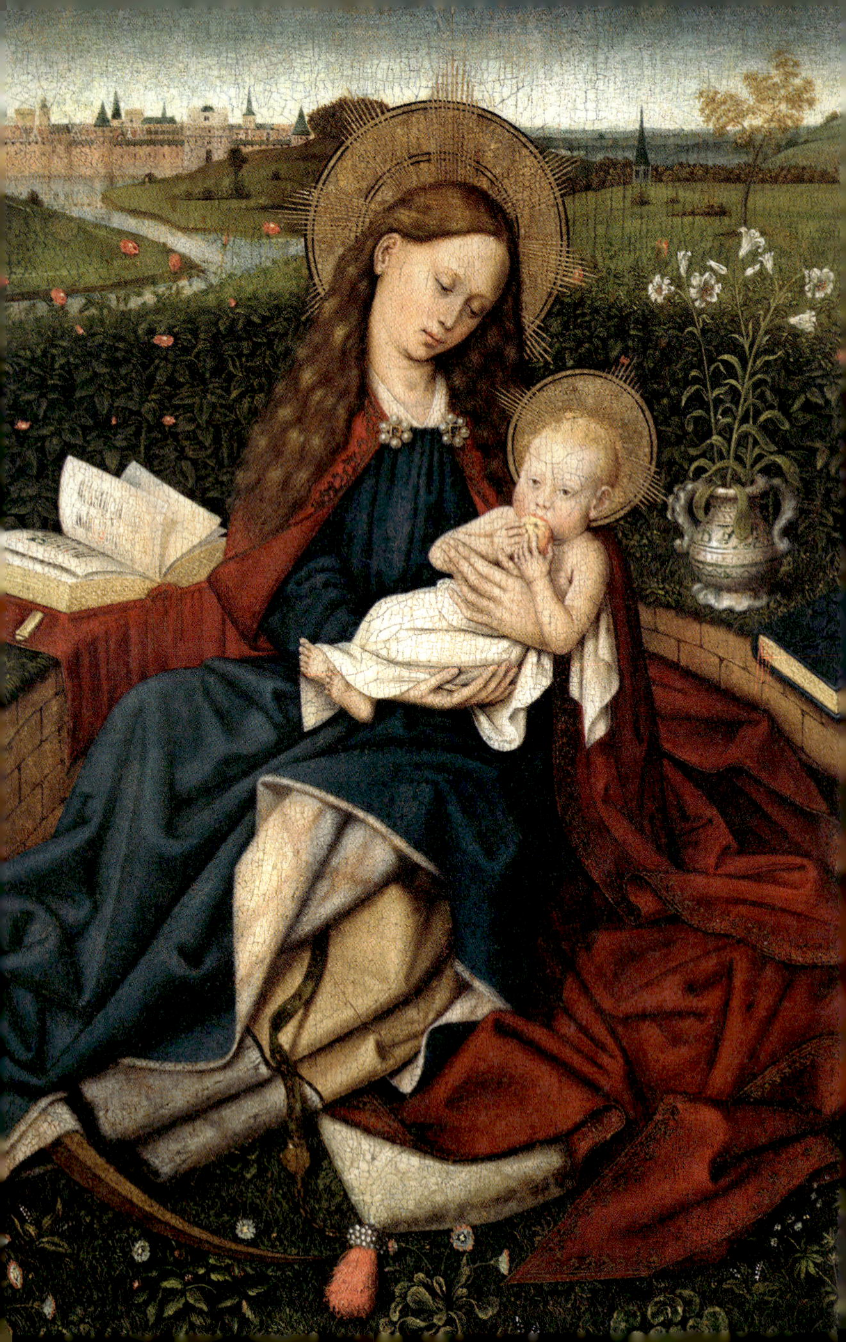

Ordinary Time

Year B

Second Sunday in Ordinary Time

1 SAMUEL 3:3B–10, 19

PSALM 40:2, 4, 7–8, 8–9, 10

1 CORINTHIANS 6:13C–15A, 17–20

JOHN 1:35–42

Hearing the Call

In the call of Samuel and the first Apostles, today's readings shed light on our own calling to be followers of Christ.

Notice in the Gospel today that John's disciples are prepared to hear God's call. They are already looking for the Messiah, so they trust in John's word and follow when he points out the Lamb of God walking by. Samuel is also waiting on the Lord—sleeping near the Ark of the Covenant where God's glory dwells, taking instruction from Eli, the high priest.

Samuel listened to God's Word and the Lord was with him. And Samuel, through his word, turned all Israel to the Lord (see 1 Samuel 3:21; 7:2–3). The disciples, too, heard and followed—words we hear repeatedly in today's Gospel. They stayed with the Lord and by their testimony brought others to the Lord.

These scenes from salvation history should give us strength to embrace God's will and to follow His call in our lives. God is constantly calling to each of us—personally, by name (see Isaiah 43:1; John 10:3). He wants us to seek Him in love, to long for His Word (see Wisdom 6:11–12). We must desire always, as the Apostles did, to stay where the Lord stays, to constantly seek His face (see Psalm 42:2). For we are not our own but belong to the Lord, as Paul says in today's Epistle.

We must have ears open to obedience and write His Word within our hearts. We must trust in the Lord's promise: if we come to Him in faith, He will abide with us (see John 15:14; 14:21–23), and raise us by His power. And we must reflect in our lives the love He has shown us so that others may find the Messiah. As we renew our vows of discipleship in this Eucharist, let us approach the altar singing the new song of today's Psalm: "Behold I come . . . to do your will O God."

Jesus takes initiative when He interacts with the disciples in this Gospel passage. He invites their free response. In cooperating with Jesus, Andrew and Peter start on their journey toward true freedom.

> The divine initiative in the work of grace precedes, prepares, and elicits the free response of man. Grace responds to the deepest yearnings of human freedom, calls freedom to cooperate with it, and perfects freedom. (CCC 2022)

Jesus is an authentic teacher. The disciples acknowledge Him as such. Authentic teachers can't help but teach, and those who follow in the footsteps of the Apostles today—the Bishop of Rome and all bishops united with him—continue offering what we are looking for: clear teaching about life, freedom, and what it means to be truly human.

The Roman Pontiff and the bishops, as authentic teachers, preach to the People of God the faith which is to be believed and applied in moral life. It is also incumbent on them to pronounce on moral questions that fall within the natural law and reason. (CCC 2050)

What does it mean to say that grace perfects freedom by calling freedom to cooperate with it?

To whom could I say "Come, and you will see"? That is, who in my community might I invite to learn more about Jesus and His Church?

SS. Peter and Andrew, you were blessed to interact with Jesus in many ways, including friendly conversation. Pray for me as I share my thoughts and feelings with Jesus in prayer, that I can experience a personal, disciple relationship with my Master and Teacher. Amen.

WE HAVE FOUND THE MESSIAH: JESUS CHRIST, WHO BRINGS US TRUTH *and* GRACE.

JOHN 1:41, 17B

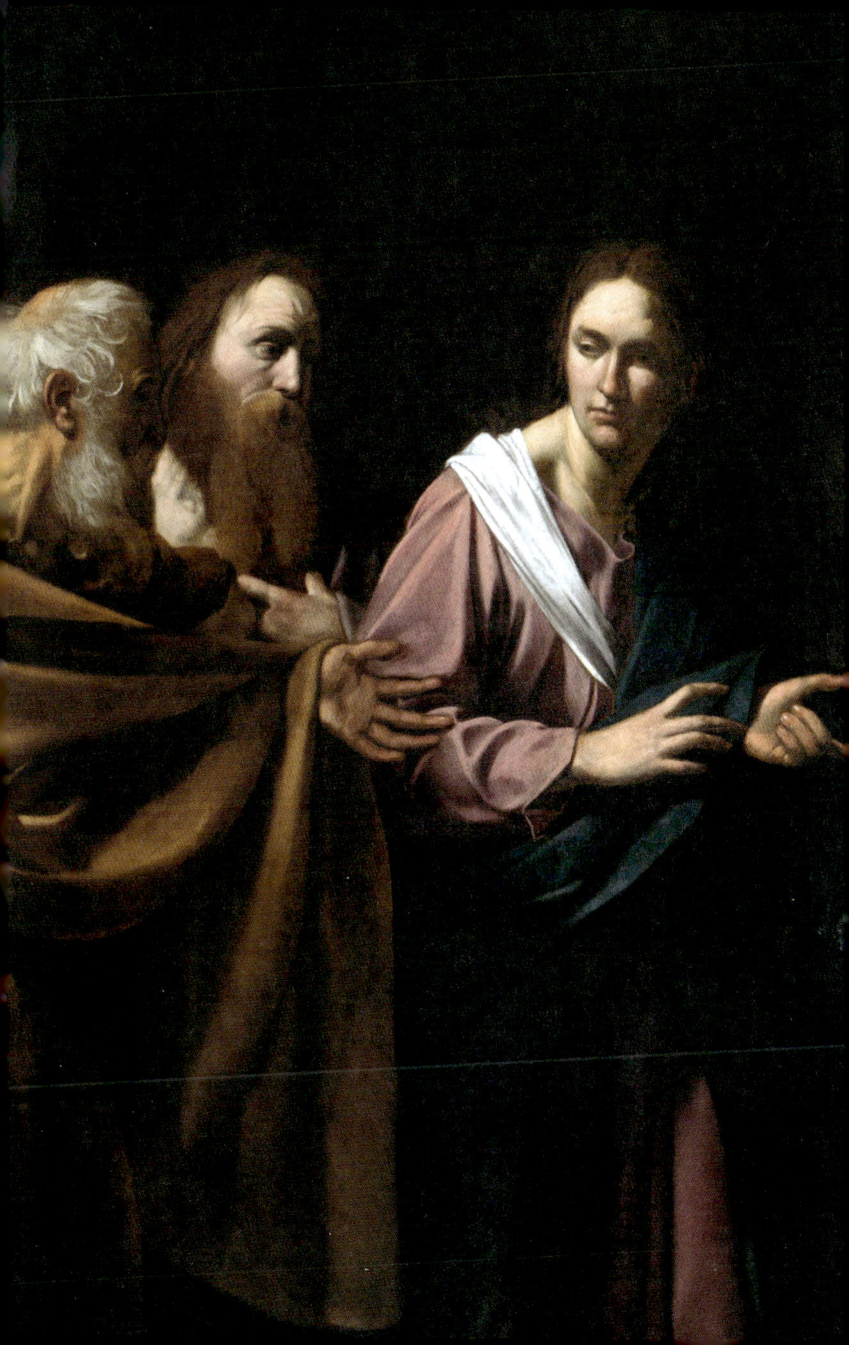

Third Sunday in Ordinary Time

JONAH 3:1–5, 10

PSALM 25:4–5, 6–7, 8–9

1 CORINTHIANS 7:29–31

MARK 1:14–20

Following Him

The calling of the brothers in today's Gospel evokes Elisha's commissioning by the prophet Elijah (see 1 Kings 19:19–21). As Elijah comes upon Elisha working on his family's farm, so Jesus sees the brothers working by the seaside. And as Elisha left his mother and father to follow Elijah, so the brothers leave their father to come after Jesus.

Jesus' promise—to make them "fishers of men"—evokes Israel's deepest hopes. The prophet Jeremiah announced a new exodus in which God would send "many fishermen" to restore the Israelites from exile, as once He brought them out of slavery in Egypt (see Jeremiah 16:14–16).

By Jesus' Cross and Resurrection, this new exodus has begun (see Luke 9:31). And the Apostles are the first of a new people of God, the Church—a new family, based not on blood ties but on belief in Jesus and a desire to do the Father's will (see John 1:12–13; Matthew 12:46–50). From now on, even our most important worldly concerns—family relations, occupations, and possessions—must be judged in light of the Gospel, Paul says in today's Epistle.

The first word of Jesus' Gospel, "repent," means we must totally change our way of thinking and living, turning from evil, doing all for the love of God. We should therefore be consoled by Nineveh's repentance in today's First Reading. Even the wicked people of Nineveh could repent at Jonah's preaching.

In Jesus, we have "something greater than Jonah" (see Matthew 12:41). We have God come as our Savior to show sinners the way, as we sing in today's Psalm. This should give us hope that loved ones who remain far from God will find compassion if they turn to Him. But we, too, must continue along the path of repentance—striving daily to pattern our lives after His.

Jesus called them. He called twelve men from among all His female and male followers. The Church that Jesus established, like Him, recognizes a suitability for priestly ministry in a small but important group of men; she, like Jesus, calls them.

> The Church confers the sacrament of Holy Orders only on baptized men (*viri*), whose suitability for the exercise of the ministry has been duly recognized. Church authority alone has the responsibility and right to call someone to receive the sacrament of Holy Orders. (CCC 1598)

They followed Him. Peter, Andrew, James, and John fulfilled "the first calling of the Christian": to listen to and follow Jesus. Zebedee did not prevent the latter two from answering Jesus' call. For all we know, he may have encouraged them. Parents must always encourage children to listen for and to answer their call from God—their vocation.

Parents should respect and encourage their children's vocations. They should remember and teach that the first calling of the Christian is to follow Jesus. (CCC 2253)

THE KINGDOM OF GOD IS AT HAND. REPENT AND BELIEVE IN THE GOSPEL.

MARK 1:15

What is Jesus' basic message?

In what ways do I or should I encourage and respect the vocations of the children in my life?

SS. James and John, you heard the call of Jesus, answering it with trust and courage. Pray for me, that I avail myself of all the ways Jesus shares His thoughts and feelings with me. Help me to hear Him calling me to live each day as His loving, trusting disciple. Amen.

Fourth Sunday in Ordinary Time

DEUTERONOMY 18:15–20

PSALM 95:1–2, 6–7, 7–9

1 CORINTHIANS 7:32–35

MARK 1:21–28

The King's Authority

Last week, Jesus announced the kingdom of God is at hand. This week, in mighty words and deeds, He exercises His dominion, asserting royal authority over the ruler of this world, Satan (see John 12:31).

Notice that today's events take place on the Sabbath. The Sabbath was to be an everlasting sign both of God's covenant love for His creation (see Exodus 20:8–11; 31:12–17) and His deliverance of his covenant people, Israel, from slavery (see Deuteronomy 6:12–15). On this Sabbath, Jesus signals a new creation—that the Holy One has come to purify His people and deliver the world from evil.

"With an unclean spirit" is biblical language for a man possessed by a demon, Satan being the prince of demons (see Mark 3:22). The demons' question: "What have you to do with us?" is often used in Old Testament scenes of combat and judgment (see Judges 11:12; 1 Kings 17:18).

And as God by His Word "rebuked" the forces of chaos in creating the world (see Psalm 104:7; Job 26:10–12) and again rebuked the Red Sea so the Israelites could make their exodus (see Psalm 106:9), Mark uses the same word to describe Jesus rebuking the demons (see Mark 4:39; Zechariah 3:2).

Jesus is the prophet foretold by Moses in today's First Reading (see Acts 3:22). Though He has authority over heaven and earth (see Daniel 7:14, 27; Revelation 12:10), He becomes one of our own kinsmen.

He comes to rebuke the forces of evil and chaos—not only in the world but in our lives. He wants to make us holy in body and spirit, as Paul says in today's Epistle (see Exodus 31:12). In this liturgy, we hear His voice and "see" His works, as we sing in today's Psalm. And as Moses tells us today, we should listen to Him.

The unclean spirit, interestingly, knew Jesus—not as a rival of God, but as someone with an entirely unique relationship to Our Father. Even a demon had sense enough to know that, ultimately, God is one.

> "Hear, O Israel, the LORD our God is one LORD . . ." (*Dt* 6:4; *Mk* 12:29). "The supreme being must be unique, without equal. . . . If God is not one, he is not God" (Tertullian, *Adv. Marc.*, 1, 3, 5: PL 2, 274). (CCC 228)

Jesus kept the Sabbath. He also had no problem using and delegating authority. The Church that Jesus founded authoritatively teaches that each and every Sunday, one way or another, Catholics had better try hard to find a way to participate in Mass.

> "Sunday . . . is to be observed as the foremost holy day of obligation in the universal Church" (CIC, can. 1246 § 1). "On Sundays

and other holy days of obligation the faithful are bound to participate in the Mass" (CIC, can. 1247). (CCC 2192)

What is my overall attitude toward legitimate authority? Keeping in mind Jesus' example of authority exercised appropriately, how might my attitude in this area improve at least a bit?

How might I be influencing my community by my example of participating in Mass every Sunday?

Heavenly Father, I acknowledge You as the loving Creator of every person, place, and thing. May the witness of my life help draw others to You. May all women and men hear Your voice, respond to Your call, and accept Your gift of salvation through Christ Our Lord. Amen.

THE PEOPLE WHO

SIT IN DARKNESS

HAVE SEEN A GREAT LIGHT;

ON THOSE DWELLING

IN A LAND

OVERSHADOWED *by* DEATH,

LIGHT HAS ARISEN.

MATTHEW 4:16

Fifth Sunday in Ordinary Time

JOB 7:1–4, 6–7

PSALM 147:1–2, 3–4, 5–6

1 CORINTHIANS 9:16–19, 22–23

MARK 1:29–39

Raised to Serve

In today's First Reading, Job describes the futility of life before Christ. His lament reminds us of the curse of toil and death placed upon Adam following his original sin (see Genesis 3:17–19). Men and women are like slaves seeking shade, unable to find rest. Their lives are like the wind that comes and goes.

But, as we sing in today's Psalm, He who created the stars promised to heal the brokenhearted and gather those lost in exile from Him (see Isaiah 11:12; 61:1). We see this promise fulfilled in today's Gospel.

Simon's mother-in-law is like Job's toiling, hopeless humanity. She is laid low by affliction, too weak to save herself. But as God promised to take His chosen people by the hand (see Isaiah 42:6), Jesus grasps her by the hand and helps her up. The word translated "help" is actually Greek for "raising up." The same verb is used when Jesus commands a dead girl to rise (see Mark 5:41–42). It's used again to describe His own Resurrection (see Mark 14:28; 16:6).

What Jesus has done for Simon's mother-in-law He has done for all humanity. He has raised all of us who lay dead through our sins (see Ephesians 2:5).

Notice all the words of totality and completeness in the Gospel. The whole town gathers; all the sick are brought to Him; He drives out demons in the whole of Galilee; everyone is looking for Christ. We, too, have found Him. By our baptism, He healed and raised us to live in His presence (see Hosea 6:1–2).

Like Simon's mother-in-law, there is only one way we can thank Him for the new life He has given us. We must rise to serve Him and His Gospel. Our lives must be our thanksgiving, as Paul describes in today's Epistle. We must tell everyone the Good News, the purpose for which Jesus has come: that others, too, may have a share in this salvation.

Jesus could have asked an Apostle to grasp Peter's mother-in-law's hand and help her up. Rather, He approached and did it Himself, just as He cured many others who were sick. In the Sacrament of the Anointing of the Sick, the priest acts in the person of Jesus, facilitating a unique encounter with our living, risen Lord.

> Only priests (presbyters and bishops) can give the sacrament of the Anointing of the Sick, using oil blessed by the bishop, or if necessary by the celebrating presbyter himself.
> (CCC 1530)

A pattern of prayer is obvious in Jesus' life. The Church He founded calls us to follow Jesus' example in various ways—establishing a healthy, holy habit of prayer.

> The Church invites the faithful to regular prayer: daily prayers, the Liturgy of the Hours,

Sunday Eucharist, the feasts of the liturgical year. (CCC 2720)

CHRIST TOOK AWAY OUR INFIRMITIES AND BORE OUR DISEASES.

MATTHEW 8:17

When do I go off to a deserted place and pray? How might I do this a bit more often?

The Liturgy of the Hours connects me with my Church community throughout the entire world. How might I learn more about this type of prayer, and consider practicing it in some form?

St. Paul, you exhort God's people to a life of gratitude. Please pray that my heart will always be thankful to God, compelling me to share with others the Good News of salvation from sin and death by the Passion, death, and Resurrection of Jesus. Amen.

Sixth Sunday in Ordinary Time

LEVITICUS 13:1–2, 44–46

PSALM 32:1–2, 5, 11

1 CORINTHIANS 10:31–11:1

MARK 1:40–45

Made Clean

In the Old Testament, leprosy is depicted as punishment for disobedience of God's commands (see Numbers 12:12–15; 2 Kings 5:27; 15:5). Considered "unclean," unfit to worship or live with the Israelites, lepers are considered "stillborn," the living dead (see Numbers 12:12). Indeed, the requirements imposed on lepers in today's First Reading—rent garments, shaven head, covered beard—are signs of death, penance, and mourning (see Leviticus 10:6; Ezekiel 24:17).

So there's more to the story in today's Gospel than a miraculous healing. When Elisha, invoking God's name, healed the leper, Naaman, it proved there was a prophet in Israel (see 2 Kings 5:8). Today's healing reveals Jesus as far more than a great prophet. He is God visiting His people (see Luke 7:16).

Only God can cure leprosy and cleanse from sin (see 2 Kings 5:7); and only God has the power to bring about what He wills (see Isaiah 55:11; Wisdom 12:18).

The Gospel scene has an almost sacramental quality about it. Jesus stretches out His hand, just as God the Father, by His outstretched arm, performed mighty deeds to save the Israelites (see Exodus 14:16; Acts 4:30). Christ's ritual sign is accompanied by a divine word, "Be made clean." And, like God's Word in creation ("Let there be"), Jesus' word "does" what He commands (see Psalm 33:9).

The same thing happens when we show ourselves to the priest in the Sacrament of Penance. On our knees like the leper, we confess our sins to the Lord, as we sing in today's

Psalm. And through the outstretched arm and divine word spoken by His priest, the Lord takes away the guilt of our sin.

Like the leper, we should rejoice in the Lord and spread the news of His mercy. We should testify to our healing by living changed lives. As Paul says in today's Epistle, we should do even the littlest things for the glory of God and that others may be saved.

Jesus knows the limitations of being a bodily person. Injury. Fatigue. Leprosy. When we call the Church Christ's Body, we tap into a deep wellspring of understanding of this great mystery. Jesus can and does heal bodies, making them clean. He offers cleansing and genuine health to us constantly—individually and as a community of persons.

> The Church is the Body of Christ. Through the Spirit and his action in the sacraments, above all the Eucharist, Christ, who once was dead and is now risen, establishes the community of believers as his own Body. (CCC 805)

"I do will it," says Jesus. He knows what it means to enjoy freedom. Would that we readily took responsibility for all of our freely chosen acts. Would that we all used our freedom as perfectly as the Son of God, who challenges us and helps us live lives in which we can take appropriate pride.

> Freedom characterizes properly human acts. It makes the human being responsible for acts of which he is the voluntary agent. His deliberate acts properly belong to him. (CCC 1745)

How am I at taking responsibility for acts of which I am the "voluntary agent"? What, if any, persistent sinful acts do I need to take to Jesus, saying, "You can make me clean"?

Lepers were outcasts in Jesus' day. Who are the societal outcasts of my community? What might I do to show genuine concern for them?

Jesus, You make Yourself available to me in the sacraments in unique and irreplaceable ways. Help me always to appreciate the healing, life-giving grace You offer sacramentally and to avail myself often of these beautiful gifts—the sacraments of Your holy Church. Amen.

A GREAT PROPHET

HAS ARISEN

IN OUR MIDST,

GOD *has* VISITED

HIS PEOPLE.

LUKE 7:16

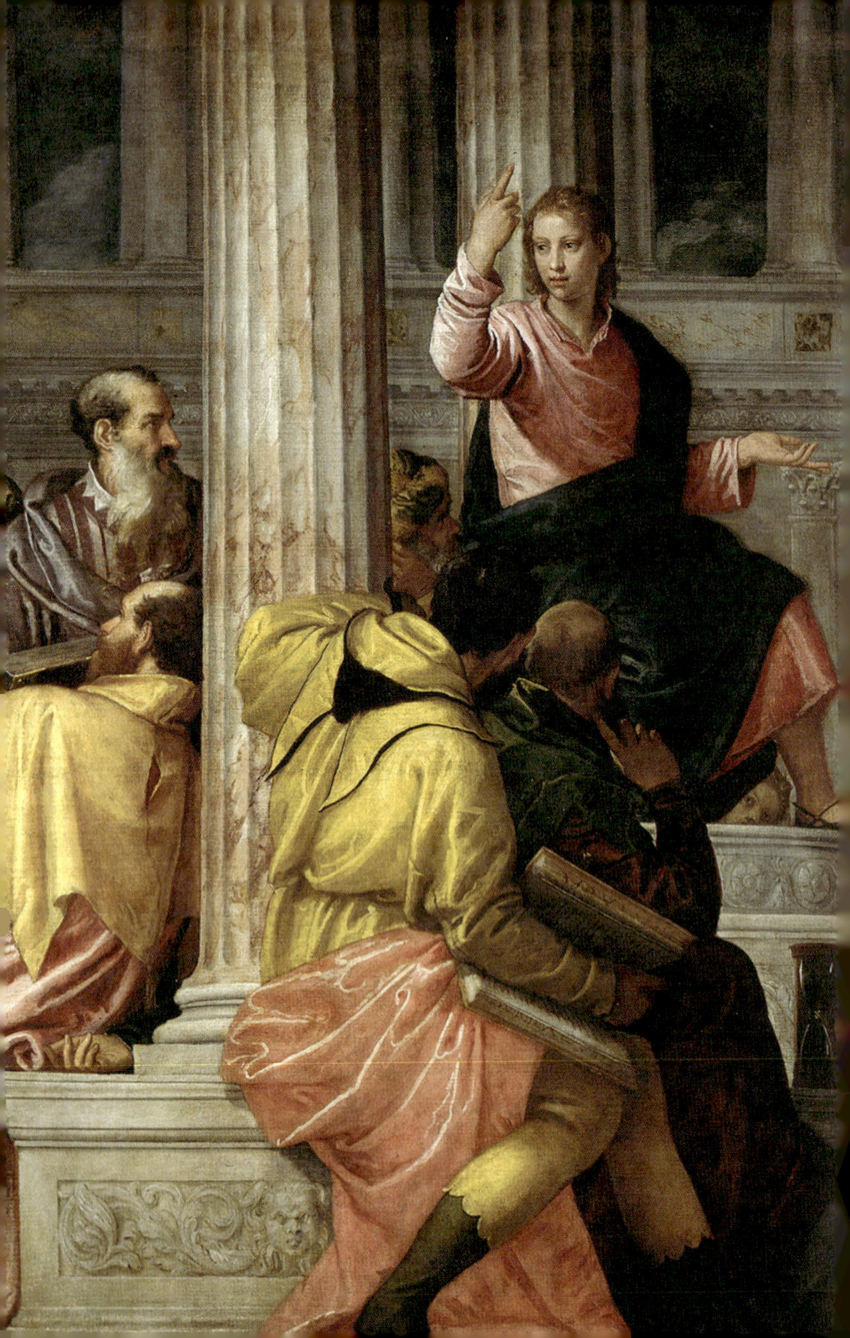

Seventh Sunday in Ordinary Time

ISAIAH 43:18–19, 21–22, 24B–25

PSALM 41:2–5, 13–14

2 CORINTHIANS 1:18–22

MARK 2:1–12

God's Great Amen

Today's Gospel makes explicit what has been implied in preceding weeks. Namely, that in healing the sick and casting out demons, Jesus is manifesting God's forgiveness of His people's sins. They had wearied of God, refusing to call on His name, we hear in today's First Reading. Despite that, God promised to remember their sins no more.

In Scripture, sin is often equated with sickness. And today's Psalm reads like a foretelling of the Gospel scene: the man is helped on his sickbed, healed of his sins, and made able to stand before the Lord forever.

The scribes know that God alone can forgive sins. That's why they accuse Jesus of blasphemy. He appears to be claiming equality with God. But the Gospel today turns on this recognition. The scene marks the first time in the Gospels that Jesus commends the faith of a person or persons who come to Him (see Matthew 9:2; Luke 5:20).

With the eyes of faith, the paralytic and his friends can see what the scribes cannot—Jesus' divine identity. He reveals Himself as the "Son of Man," alluding to the mysterious heavenly figure the prophet Daniel saw receive kingship over all the earth (see Daniel 7:13–14). His retort to the scribes even echoes what God said to Pharaoh when He sent plagues upon Egypt: "That you may know that I am the Lord" (see Exodus 8:19; 9:14).

As Paul says in today's Epistle, Jesus is God's great Amen. Amen means "so be it." In Jesus, God has said, "so be it," fulfilling all His promises throughout salvation history.

We are the new people He formed to announce His praise. He calls each of us what Jesus calls the paralytic: His child (see 2 Corinthians 6:18). But do we share this man's faith? To what lengths are we willing to go to encounter Jesus? How much are we willing to sacrifice so that our friends, too, might hear His saving word?

The four men carrying the paralytic had a goal. They chose an alternate means of reaching their end, and, presuming they fixed the roof afterward, one could assert that they performed a morally good act. Both a good goal and a good method, as well as circumstances permitting sufficient knowledge and freedom, are required to call an act morally good.

> A morally good act requires the goodness of its object, of its end, and of its circumstances together. (CCC 1760)

Jesus didn't hang up a sign saying "Entry through Door Only." He didn't expressly reveal a preferred way of proceeding in this case. At other times, Jesus did articulate ordinary means of behavior, and His Church occasionally does so as well, expressing God's wishes with as much certainty as feasible this side of heaven. The way that mortal sin is addressed is one of these instances.

Individual and integral confession of grave sins followed by absolution remains the only ordinary means of reconciliation with God and with the Church. (CCC 1497)

What are some of the ordinary means—the usual ways—God has revealed for expressing and living out the faith? (This phrase often refers to sacraments and matters related to them.)

How would I explain the Sacrament of Penance to one who thinks it's unnecessary? (Hint: the phrase "ordinary means" may come in handy.)

Jesus, the Sacrament of Penance is a special gift from You to me. I know that I fall short at times, succumbing to temptation and sin. Give me the courage and humility to celebrate this sacrament often, seeking You out for the healing of my soul and the grace to resist temptation, avoiding sin by Your mercy. Amen.

THE LORD SENT ME

TO BRING GLAD TIDINGS

TO THE POOR,

and TO PROCLAIM

LIBERTY TO CAPTIVES.

CF. LUKE 4:18

Eighth Sunday in Ordinary Time

HOSEA 2:16B, 17B, 21–22

PSALM 103:1–2, 3–4, 8, 10, 12–13

2 CORINTHIANS 3:1B–6

MARK 2:18–22

With the Bridegroom

Today's readings draw on an ancient biblical theme: the image of God as divine bridegroom of His beloved Israel and the covenant as a divine–human wedding pact (see Isaiah 61:10; 62:4–5).

In the First Reading, God, speaking through the prophet Hosea, recalls Israel's exodus and sojourn in the wilderness as a time of betrothal in which He spoke to their heart and they responded in love (see Deuteronomy 7:6–8).

He promises a new day when He will again take His bride to the desert. On that day, He vows, despite Israel's adultery, its faithlessness to the covenant (see Jeremiah 2:20; 3:8), He will wed His bride forever. He vows to make a new covenant (see Hosea 2:20) and, using a term of marital intimacy, promises that Israel shall "know" the Lord (see Genesis 4:1).

This tradition is behind Jesus' description of Himself as "the bridegroom" in today's Gospel. At the time, "bridegroom" was not a term that Israelites used to describe their expected Messiah. So Jesus, again, as in all the Gospel texts in recent weeks, is being revealed as God (see John 2:1–12; 3:29; Matthew 22:1–14; 25:1–13).

In His mercy, He has redeemed our lives from the destruction of sin, as we sing in today's Psalm. This is the new covenant that Paul speaks of in today's Epistle. It is a covenant written not on stone tablets as the old covenant law was but on our hearts (see Jeremiah 31:33).

Today's readings remind us that we have been betrothed to Christ in Baptism (see 2 Corinthians 11:2), cleansed by the bath of water and the Word and called to remain holy and without blemish (see Ephesians 5:25–27) until the heavenly wedding feast at the end of time (see Revelation 19:7–9). We anticipate that feast in each Mass, drinking the wine of the new covenant made in His blood (see Zechariah 9:16–17; Isaiah 25:6; Luke 22:20).

Jesus seems fond of weddings. How fitting, then, that one way of grasping the mystery that is our Church is to consider her as the Bride of Christ.

> The Church is the Bride of Christ: he loved her and handed himself over for her. He has purified her by his blood and made her the fruitful mother of all God's children. (CCC 808)

Our bridegroom, Jesus, is with us at every liturgy. We do not fast at the Eucharistic liturgy; we are fed there. Liturgy helps strengthen us to live morally as friends of Jesus Christ—to understand and act upon our Church's precepts and other moral teachings.

The precepts of the Church concern the moral and Christian life united with the liturgy and nourished by it. (CCC 2048)

THE FATHER WILLED TO GIVE US BIRTH BY THE WORD OF TRUTH THAT WE MAY BE A KIND OF FIRSTFRUITS OF HIS CREATURES.

JAMES 1:18

To what degree is my life as a Christian united with the liturgy and nourished by it? How might I make a positive adjustment here?

Do I know any newly married couples who could benefit from my prayerful support? How might I encourage one or more recently married couples?

Jesus, I know that the Church is Your Mystical Body and spotless Bride. Help me always to live my personal, disciple relationship with You in full communion with Your holy Church. Amen.

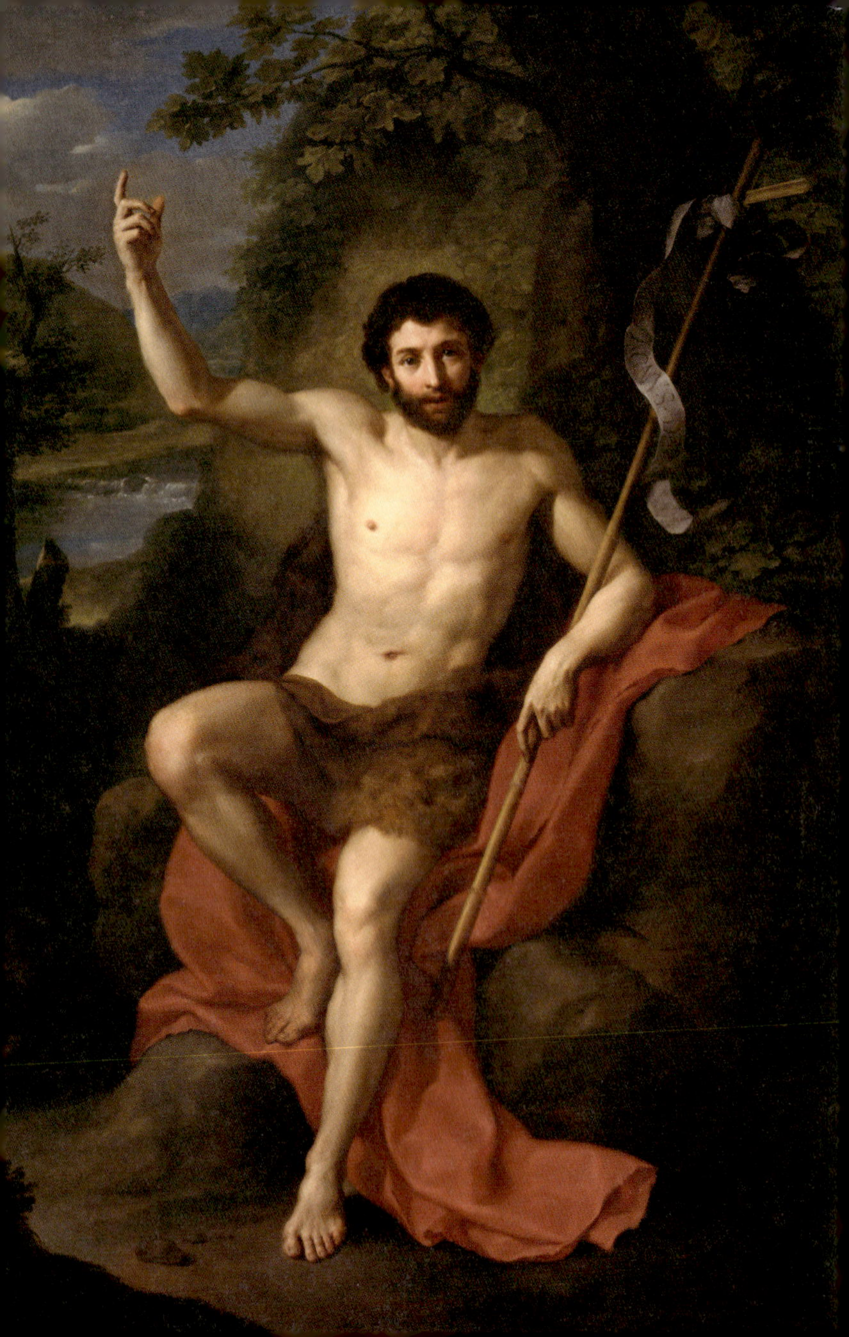

Lent

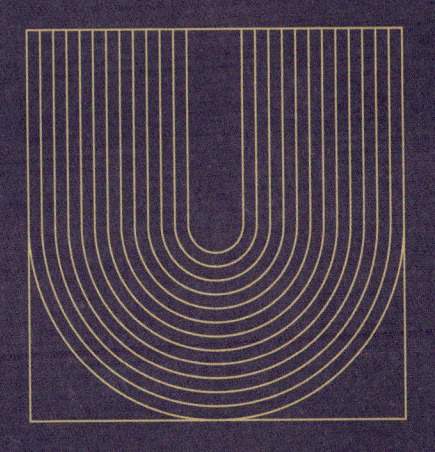

Year B

First Sunday of Lent

GENESIS 9:8–15

PSALM 25:4–5, 6–7, 8–9

1 PETER 3:18–22

MARK 1:12–15

The New Creation

Lent bids us to return to the innocence of Baptism. As Noah and his family were saved through the waters of the deluge, we were saved through the waters of Baptism, Peter reminds us in today's Epistle.

And God's covenant with Noah in today's First Reading marked the start of a new world. But it also prefigured a new and greater covenant between God and His creation (see Hosea 2:20; Isaiah 11:1–9).

We see that new covenant and that new creation begin in today's Gospel. Jesus is portrayed as the New Adam—the beloved Son of God (see Mark 1:11; Luke 3:38) living in harmony with the wild beasts (see Genesis 2:19–20), being served by angels (see Ezekiel 28:12–14). Like Adam, He is tempted by the devil. But while Adam fell, giving reign to sin and death, Jesus is victorious (see Romans 5:12–14, 17–20).

This is the Good News, the "gospel of God" that He proclaims. Through His death, Resurrection, and enthronement at the right hand of the Father, the world is once again made God's kingdom.

In the waters of Baptism, each of us entered the kingdom of His beloved Son (see Colossians 1:13–14). We were made children of God, new creations (see 2 Corinthians 5:17; Galatians 4:3–7). But like Jesus, and Israel before Him, we have passed through the baptismal waters only to be driven into the wilderness, a world filled with afflictions and tests of our faithfulness (see 1 Corinthians 10:1–4, 9, 13; Deuteronomy 8:2, 16).

We are led on this journey by Jesus. He is the Savior, the way and the truth we sing of in today's Psalm (see John 14:6). He feeds us with the bread of angels (see Psalm 78:25; Wisdom 16:20) and cleanses our consciences in the Sacrament of Reconciliation. As we begin this holy season, let us renew our baptismal vows to repent and believe in the Gospel.

In the Church year, or liturgical calendar, Lent marks a time between early Ordinary Time and the observance of Jesus' death, Resurrection, and Ascension. When we are mindful of the liturgical year, we are mindful of the life, teaching, and actions of Jesus. Our Church year helps us journey with and get to know the Lord better and better as the years pass.

> The Church, "in the course of the year, . . . unfolds the whole mystery of Christ from his Incarnation and Nativity through his Ascension, to Pentecost and the expectation of the blessed hope of the coming of the Lord" (SC 102 § 2). (CCC 1194)

Jesus uses His freedom wisely and well. He expects us to respect others' freedom and to use ours in the service of God's kingdom. When we abuse this freedom, we are to repent and recommit ourselves to the Good News of our salvation in Him. We are called to believe in the Gospel.

> The right to the exercise of freedom, especially in religious and moral matters, is an inalienable requirement of the dignity of man. But the exercise of freedom does not entail the putative right to say or do anything. (CCC 1747)

How am I at avoiding near occasions of sin—those times when I drive myself to the desert of temptation?

In my communities, do I use my freedom responsibly or take it as right to do and say anything?

Holy Spirit, You led Jesus through a period of fasting and prayer. Guide me throughout this Lenten season as I strive to deepen my experience of repentance as well as strengthen my faith in the Good News of salvation. Amen.

ONE DOES NOT LIVE

ON BREAD ALONE,

BUT ON EVERY WORD

THAT COMES FORTH

FROM THE MOUTH *of* GOD.

MATTHEW 4:4B

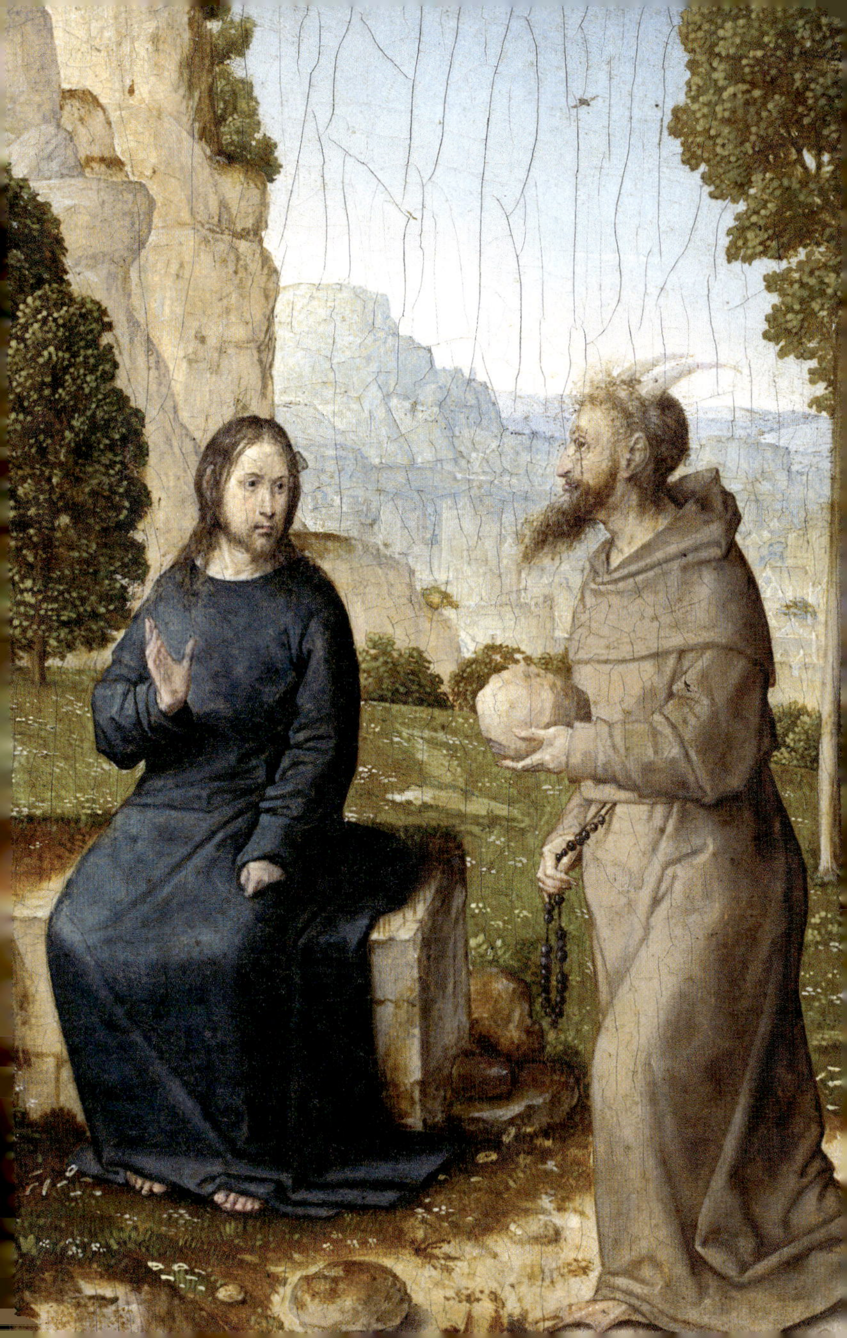

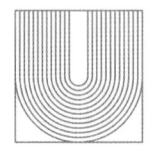

Second Sunday of Lent

GENESIS 22:1–2, 9A, 10–13, 15–18

PSALM 116:10, 15, 16–17, 18–19

ROMANS 8:31B–34

MARK 9:2–10

Bonds Loosed

The Lenten season continues with another story of testing. Last Sunday, we heard the trial of Jesus in the desert. In this week's First Reading, we hear of how Abraham was put to the test.

The Church has always read this story as a sign of God's love for the world in giving His only begotten Son. In today's Epistle, Paul uses exact words drawn from this story to describe how God, like Abraham, did not withhold His only Son but handed Him over for us on the Cross (see Romans 8:32; Genesis 22:12, 16).

In the Gospel today, too, we hear another echo. Jesus is called God's "beloved Son," just as Isaac is described as Abraham's beloved firstborn son. These readings are given to us in Lent to reveal Christ's identity and to strengthen us in the face of our afflictions.

Jesus is shown to be the true Son that Abraham rejoiced to see (see Matthew 1:1; John 8:56). In His Transfiguration, He is revealed to be the "prophet like Moses" foretold by God—raised from among their own kinsmen, speaking with God's own authority (see Deuteronomy 18:15, 19).

Like Moses, He climbs the mountain with three named friends and beholds God's glory in a cloud (see Exodus 24:1, 9, 15). He is the one prophesied to come after Elijah's return (see Sirach 48:9–10; Malachi 3:1, 23–24). And, as He discloses to the Apostles, He is the Son of Man sent to suffer and die for our sins (see Isaiah 53:3).

As we sing in today's Psalm, Jesus believed in the face of His afflictions, and God loosed Him from the bonds of death (see Psalm 116:3). His rising should give us the courage to face our trials, to offer ourselves totally to the Father—as He did, as Abraham and Isaac did. Freed from death by His death, we come to this Mass to offer the sacrifice of thanksgiving and to renew our vows as His servants and faithful ones.

Sometimes we take the Resurrection for granted. To Peter, James, and John, Jesus talking about the Son of Man rising from the dead must have sounded utterly mysterious. Yet, rise from the dead He did—paving the way for us all.

> Christ, "the first-born from the dead" (*Col* 1:18), is the principle of our own resurrection, even now by the justification of our souls (cf. *Rom* 6:4), and one day by the new life he will impart to our bodies (cf. *Rom* 8:11). (CCC 658)

Jesus rightfully instructed the three to keep the Transfiguration a secret, at least for the time being. Although exceptions of course occur, there are times when keeping secrets is absolutely the right thing to do.

"The sacramental seal is inviolable" (CIC, can. 983 § 1). Professional secrets must be kept. Confidences prejudicial to another are not to be divulged. (CCC 2511)

FROM THE SHINING CLOUD THE FATHER'S VOICE IS HEARD: THIS IS MY BELOVED SON, LISTEN TO HIM.

CF. MATTHEW 17:5

How good am I at remaining silent when the situation implies that it's the most appropriate course of action?

How susceptible am I to the urge to gossip? What might I do to maintain better control of my conversations in this regard?

Heavenly Father, Your love for me is so deep that You sent Your only begotten Son to suffer, die, and rise—all so that I can be happy with You forever in heaven. May my love for You grow in this Lenten season, and may my life become a truer sacrifice of thanksgiving to You. Amen.

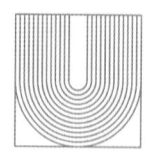

Third Sunday of Lent

EXODUS 20:1–17

PSALM 19:8, 9, 10, 11

1 CORINTHIANS 1:22–25

JOHN 2:13–25

Spiritual Sacrifices

Jesus does not come to destroy the temple but to fulfill it (see Matthew 5:17)—to reveal its true purpose in God's saving plan.

He is the Lord the prophets said would come to purify the temple, banish the merchants, and make it a house of prayer for all people (see Zechariah 14:21; Malachi 3:1–5; Isaiah 56:7). The God who made the heavens and the earth, who brought Israel out of slavery, does not dwell in sanctuaries made by human hands (see Acts 7:48; 2 Samuel 7:5). Nor does He need offerings of oxen, sheep, or doves (see Psalm 50:7–13).

Notice in today's First Reading that God did not originally command animal sacrifices, only that Israel heed His commandments (see Jeremiah 7:21–23; Amos 5:25).

His law was a gift of divine wisdom, as we sing in today's Psalm. It was a law of love (see Matthew 22:36–40), perfectly expressed in Christ's self-offering on the Cross (see John 15:13). This is the "sign" Jesus offers in the Gospel today—the sign that caused Jewish leaders to stumble, as Paul tells us in the Epistle.

Jesus' body—destroyed on the Cross and raised up three days later—is the new and true sanctuary. From the temple of His body rivers of living water flow, the Spirit of grace that makes each of us a temple (see 1 Corinthians 3:16) and together builds us into a dwelling place of God (see Ephesians 2:22).

In the Eucharist, we participate in His offering of His Body and Blood. This is the worship in Spirit and in truth that the Father desires (see John 4:23–24). We are to offer praise as our sacrifice (see Psalm 50:14, 23). This means imitating Christ—offering our bodies, all our intentions, and our and actions in every circumstance—for the love of God and the love of others (see Hebrews 10:5–7; Romans 12:1; 1 Peter 2:5).

Jesus needed no one to explain human nature to Him. He experienced human nature firsthand. And even though He got annoyed at people occasionally (clearing the temple wasn't exactly a warm and fuzzy thing to do), Jesus loves each of us infinitely and wants us all to share the divine life of our Triune God—Father, Son, and Holy Spirit.

> The Word became flesh to make us *"partakers of the divine nature"*: "For this is why the Word became man, and the Son of God became the Son of man: so that man, by entering into communion with the Word and thus receiving divine sonship, might become a son of God." "For the Son of God became man so that we might become God." "The only-begotten Son of God, wanting to make us sharers in his divinity, assumed our nature, so that he, made man, might make men gods." (CCC 460, quoting 2 Peter 1:4; St. Irenaeus, *Adv. haeres.* 3, 19, 1: PG 7/1, 939; St. Athanasius, *De inc.* 54, 3: PG 25, 192B; St. Thomas Aquinas, *Opusc.* 57, 1–4)

The vendors and currency exchangers weren't showing good judgment by plying their trade within the temple area. They weren't being fair or loving to God, in a sense, by taking up His space. The Lord doesn't mind us working for a living, nor does He forbid buying and selling what we need. He insists, though, that we be charitable and just in doing so.

> The seventh commandment enjoins the practice of justice and charity in the administration of earthly goods and the fruits of men's labor. (CCC 2451)

GOD SO LOVED THE WORLD
THAT HE GAVE HIS ONLY SON,
SO THAT EVERYONE WHO BELIEVES IN
HIM MIGHT HAVE ETERNAL LIFE.

JOHN 3:16

How good am I at being assertive (like Jesus clearing the temple) without being aggressive (saying intentionally hurtful things or initiating physical harm)?

Fairness and love should characterize my behavior as an employee, employer, customer, vendor, etc. How charitable and just am I in my daily business and temporal affairs?

Jesus, my prayers of praise, petition, and intercession reflect my love for You and my concern for family, friends, and neighbors. Hear my prayers, Lord Jesus! Grant them if they serve the salvation of souls and glorify You, who live and reign with the Father and the Holy Spirit. Amen.

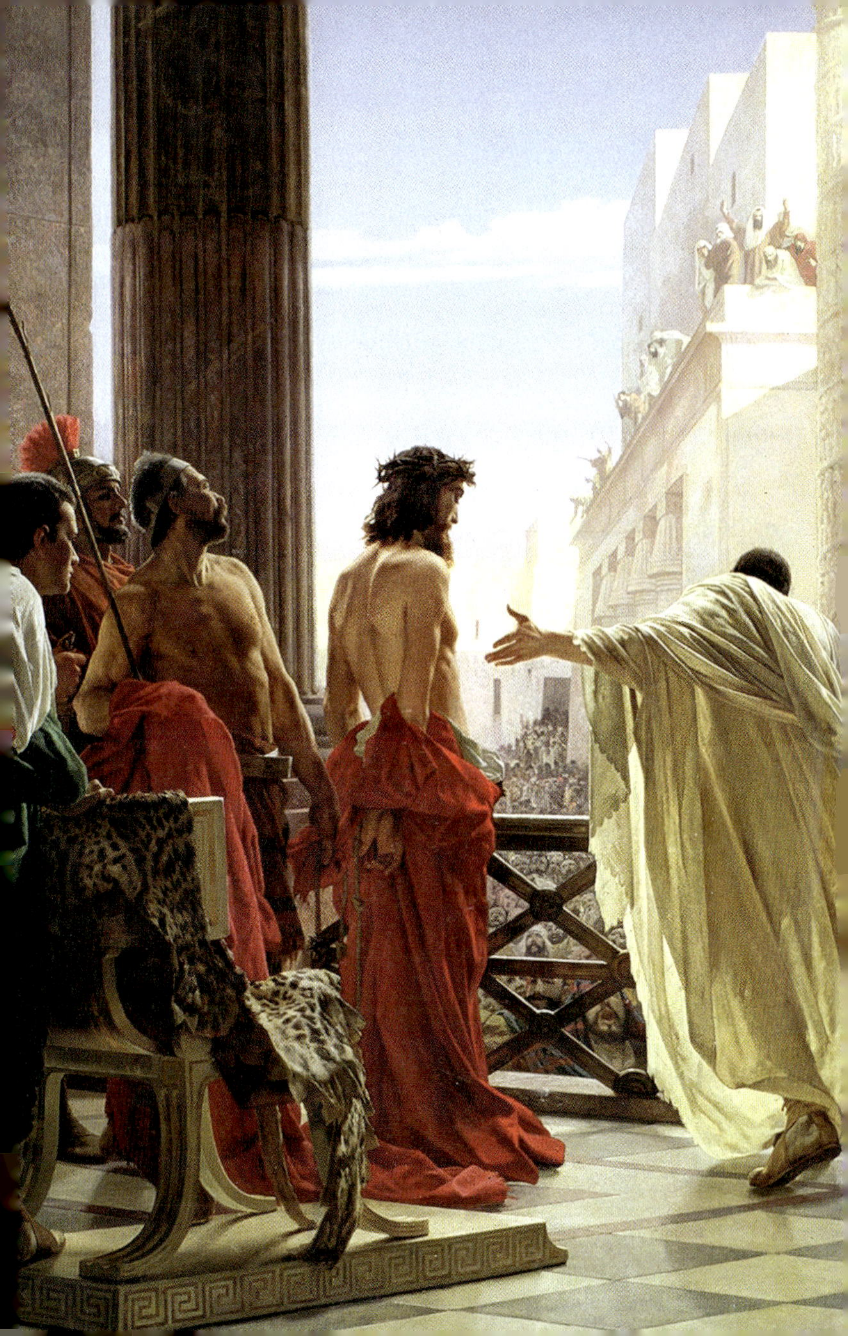

Fourth Sunday of Lent

2 CHRONICLES 36:14–16, 19–23

PSALM 137:1–2, 3, 4–5, 6

EPHESIANS 2:4–10

JOHN 3:14–21

Living in the Light

The Sunday readings in Lent have been showing us the high points of salvation history: God's covenant with creation in the time of Noah, His promises to Abraham, the law He gave to Israel at Sinai. But in today's First Reading, we hear of the destruction of the kingdom established by God's final Old Testament covenant, the covenant with David (see 2 Samuel 7; Psalm 89:3).

His chosen people abandoned the law He gave them. For their sins, the temple was destroyed, and they were exiled in Babylon. We hear their sorrow and repentance in the exile lament we sing as today's Psalm. But we also hear how God, in His mercy, gathered them back, even anointing a pagan king to shepherd them and rebuild the temple (see Isaiah 44:28–45:1, 4).

God is rich in mercy, as today's Epistle teaches. He promised that David's kingdom would last forever, that David's son would be His Son and rule all nations (see 2 Samuel 7:14–15; Psalm 2:7–9). In Jesus, God keeps that promise (see Revelation 22:16).

Moses lifted up the serpent as a sign of salvation (see Wisdom 16:5–7; Numbers 21:9). Now Jesus is lifted up on the Cross to draw all people to Himself (see John 12:32). Those who refuse to believe in this sign of the Father's love condemn themselves—as the Israelites in their infidelity brought judgment upon themselves.

But God did not leave Israel in exile, and He does not want to leave any of us dead in our transgressions. We are God's handiwork, saved to live as His people in the light of His truth. Midway through this season of repentance, let us again behold the Pierced One (see John 19:37), and rededicate ourselves to living the "good works" that God has prepared us for.

God wants no person to suffer eternal punishment. He's not out to get anyone in a negative sense. Rather, God wants us all to enjoy eternal life. And you can help.

> It is from God's love for all men that the Church in every age receives both the obligation and the vigor of her missionary dynamism, "for the love of Christ urges us on." Indeed, God "desires all men to be saved and to come to the knowledge of the truth"; that is, God wills the salvation of everyone through the knowledge of the truth. Salvation is found in the truth. Those who obey the prompting of the Spirit of truth are already on the way of salvation. But the Church, to whom this truth has been entrusted, must go out to meet their desire, so as to bring them the truth. Because she believes in God's universal plan of salvation, the Church must be missionary. (CCC 851)

Sometimes we seem to prefer darkness to the light of Our Lord. Sometimes our works are evil. Sometimes we do wicked things.

God wants us to avoid sin; this includes recognizing it for what it is. This is the first step toward rising above it, borne on the grace of God, to the saving light that is Jesus.

> Sin is an utterance, a deed, or a desire contrary to the eternal law (St. Augustine, *Faust* 22: PL 42, 418). It is an offense against God. It rises up against God in a disobedience contrary to the obedience of Christ. (CCC 1871)

GOD SO LOVED THE WORLD THAT HE GAVE HIS ONLY SON, SO THAT EVERYONE WHO BELIEVES IN HIM MIGHT HAVE ETERNAL LIFE.

JOHN 3:16

How might I describe my quest for knowledge of the truth?

What is my level of missionary dynamism? How hard do I work at lovingly helping others come to the knowledge of the truth so that through it they might enjoy salvation?

St. Augustine, you were no stranger to sin, especially in your younger years. Please pray for me so that I, like you, will answer God's call to repentance and rest in the comfort of His mercy. Amen.

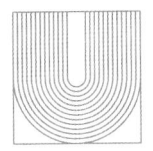

Fifth Sunday of Lent

JEREMIAH 31:31–34

PSALM 51:3–4, 12–13, 14–15

HEBREWS 5:7–9

JOHN 12:20–33

The Hour Comes

Our readings today are filled with anticipation. The days are coming, Jeremiah prophesies in today's First Reading. The hour has come, Jesus says in the Gospel. The new covenant that God promised to Jeremiah is made in the "hour" of Jesus—in His death, Resurrection, and Ascension to the Father's right hand.

The prophets said this new covenant would return Israel's exiled tribes from the ends of the world (see Jeremiah 31:1, 3–4, 7–8). Jesus, too, predicted His Passion would gather the dispersed children of God (see John 11:52). But today, He promises to draw to Himself not only Israelites but all men and women.

The new covenant is more than a political or national restoration. As we sing in today's Psalm, it is a universal spiritual restoration. In the "hour" of Jesus, sinners in every nation can return to the Father to be washed of their guilt and given new hearts to love and serve Him.

In predicting He will be "lifted up," Jesus isn't describing only His coming Crucifixion (see John 3:14–15). Isaiah used the same word to tell how the Messiah, after suffering for Israel's sins, would be raised high and greatly exalted (see Isaiah 52:13). Elsewhere, the term describes how kings are elevated above their subjects (see 1 Maccabees 8:13).

Troubled in His agony, Jesus didn't pray to be saved. Instead, as we hear in today's Epistle, He offered Himself to the Father on the Cross as a living prayer and supplication.

For this, God gave Him dominion over heaven and earth (see Acts 2:33; Philippians 2:9).

Where He has gone we can follow—if we let Him lead us. To follow Jesus means hating our lives of sin and selfishness. It means trusting in the Father's will, the law He has written in our hearts. Jesus' "hour" continues in the Eucharist, where we join our sacrifices to His, giving God our lives in reverence and obedience, confident He will raise us up to bear fruits of holiness.

Preserving your life for eternity. Once you've really heard the Good News of salvation through Jesus, it's important to become and remain a member of His Body in the ways revealed by God. Through initiation into the Christian community, you embark on and remain faithful through your journey in this world and on to eternal life.

> Christian initiation is accomplished by three sacraments together: Baptism which is the beginning of new life; Confirmation which is its strengthening; and the Eucharist which nourishes the disciple with Christ's Body and Blood for his transformation in Christ. (CCC 1275)

Whoever serves Jesus must follow Him. Serving Jesus often means making decisions guided by conscience. Following Jesus may occasionally mean making judgments that require some sacrifice.

It's true that there is no higher authority than your informed conscience. You really must inform your conscience with God's Word in Scripture and the teaching of His Church; that way, in your judgments you'll be more certain to serve and follow Jesus and, even if sacrificing, you will produce much fruit.

> A human being must always obey the certain judgment of his conscience. (CCC 1800)

> **WHOEVER SERVES ME MUST FOLLOW ME, SAYS THE LORD; AND WHERE I AM, THERE ALSO WILL MY SERVANT BE.**
>
> JOHN 12:26
>
> In what ways can a person gain life by dying? How by sacrificing greatly can I gain something even greater in return?
>
> Into what groups have I been initiated or otherwise formally received? What does this teach me about

the three sacraments of Christian initiation? What are the similarities and differences in the initiation processes?

Holy Spirit, You touch our hearts in the Sacraments of Initiation: Baptism, Confirmation, and the Most Holy Eucharist. Renew in me an appreciation for these opportunities to encounter Jesus. Help me also to set an excellent example for all catechumens as they eagerly anticipate the approaching Easter Vigil. Amen.

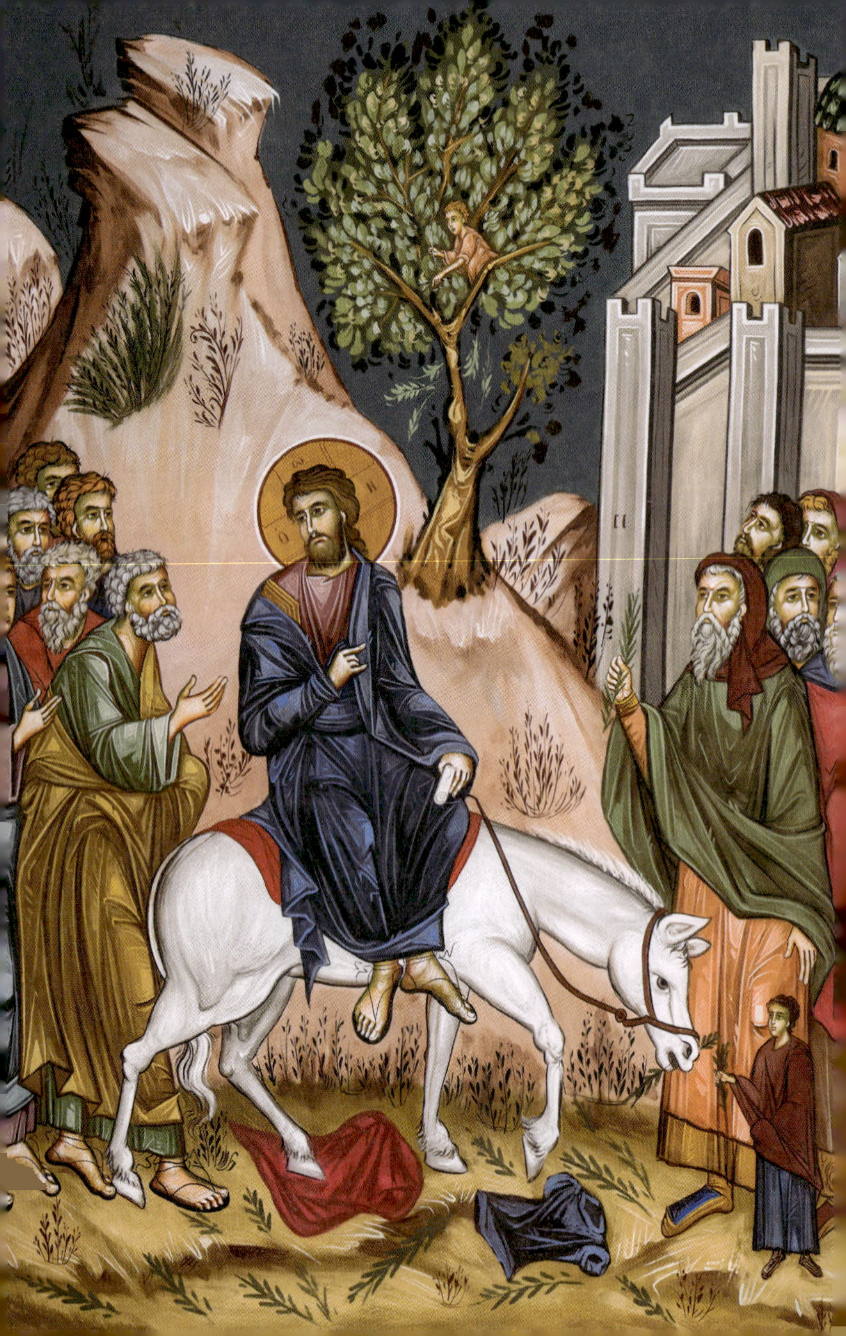

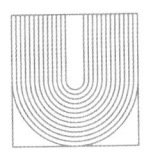

Palm Sunday of the Lord's Passion

ISAIAH 50:4–7

PSALMS 22:8–9, 17–18, 19–20, 23–24

PHILIPPIANS 2:6–11

MARK 14:1–15:47

Darkness at Noon

Crowned with thorns, Our Lord is lifted up on the Cross, where He dies as "King of the Jews." Notice how many times He is called "king" in today's Gospel—mostly in scorn and mockery. As we hear the long accounts of His Passion, at every turn we must remind ourselves that He suffered this cruel and unusual violence for us.

He is the Suffering Servant foretold by Isaiah in today's First Reading. He reenacts the agony described in today's Psalm and even dies with the first words of that Psalm on His lips (see Psalm 22:1).

Listen carefully for the echoes of this Psalm throughout today's Gospel. Jesus is beaten; His hands and feet are pierced; His enemies gamble for His clothes, wagging their heads, mocking His faith in God's love, His faith that God will deliver Him.

Are we that much different from Our Lord's tormenters? Often, don't we deny that He is king, refusing to obey His only commands that we love Him and one another? Don't we render Him mock tribute, pay Him lip service with our half-hearted devotions?

In the dark noon of Calvary, the veil in Jerusalem's temple is torn. It is a sign that by His death Jesus has destroyed forever the barrier separating us from the presence of God.

He was God and yet humbled Himself to come among us, we're reminded in today's Epistle. And despite our repeated failures, our frailty, Jesus still humbles Himself to come to us, offering us His Body and Blood in the Eucharist.

His enemies never understood that His kingship isn't of this world (see John 18:36). He wants to write His law, His rule of life, on our hearts and minds. As we enter Holy Week, let us once more resolve to give Him dominion in our lives. Let us take up the cross He gives to us and confess with all our hearts, minds, and strength that truly this is the Son of God.

The centurion makes an act of faith. He is not alone, nor is he standing with Jesus only. This centurion is surrounded by saints and sinners, by those who believe in Jesus and those who, God-willing, might believe at some future point. The centurion's expression of belief occurs within a community.

> "Believing" is an ecclesial act. The Church's faith precedes, engenders, supports and nourishes our faith. The Church is the mother of all believers. "No one can have God as Father who does not have the Church as Mother" (St. Cyprian, *De unit.* 6: PL 4, 519). (CCC 181)

It's all too easy to vilify those involved with Jesus' death. And granted, some of these agents may well have been acting with consciously evil intent. Others, though, may honestly not have known better. Some, maybe a soldier or two, may have felt forced or fearful if they didn't comply. While we can certainly judge the goodness or badness of an act (e.g., putting a man to death), we must be careful about presuming that all perpetrators always do so knowingly and willingly enough to be morally responsible in all cases.

> The imputability or responsibility for an action can be diminished or nullified by ignorance, duress, fear, and other psychological or social factors. (CCC 1746)

> CHRIST BECAME OBEDIENT
> TO THE POINT OF DEATH,
> EVEN DEATH ON A CROSS.
> BECAUSE OF THIS, GOD GREATLY
> EXALTED HIM AND BESTOWED
> ON HIM THE NAME WHICH
> IS ABOVE EVERY NAME.
>
> PHILIPPIANS 2:8–9
>
> To what extent is my faith an ecclesial act, one that occurs in the context of our Church?

How much do I allow for the possibility of ignorance, duress, fear, or other factors when considering the misdeeds of others?

Most Blessed Virgin Mary, you above all others understood the painful consequences of sin as you watched your Son suffer for the transgressions of the world. Pray for me, Blessed Mother, that the sorrow I feel this Holy Week helps motivate me to avoid all near occasions of sin. Amen.

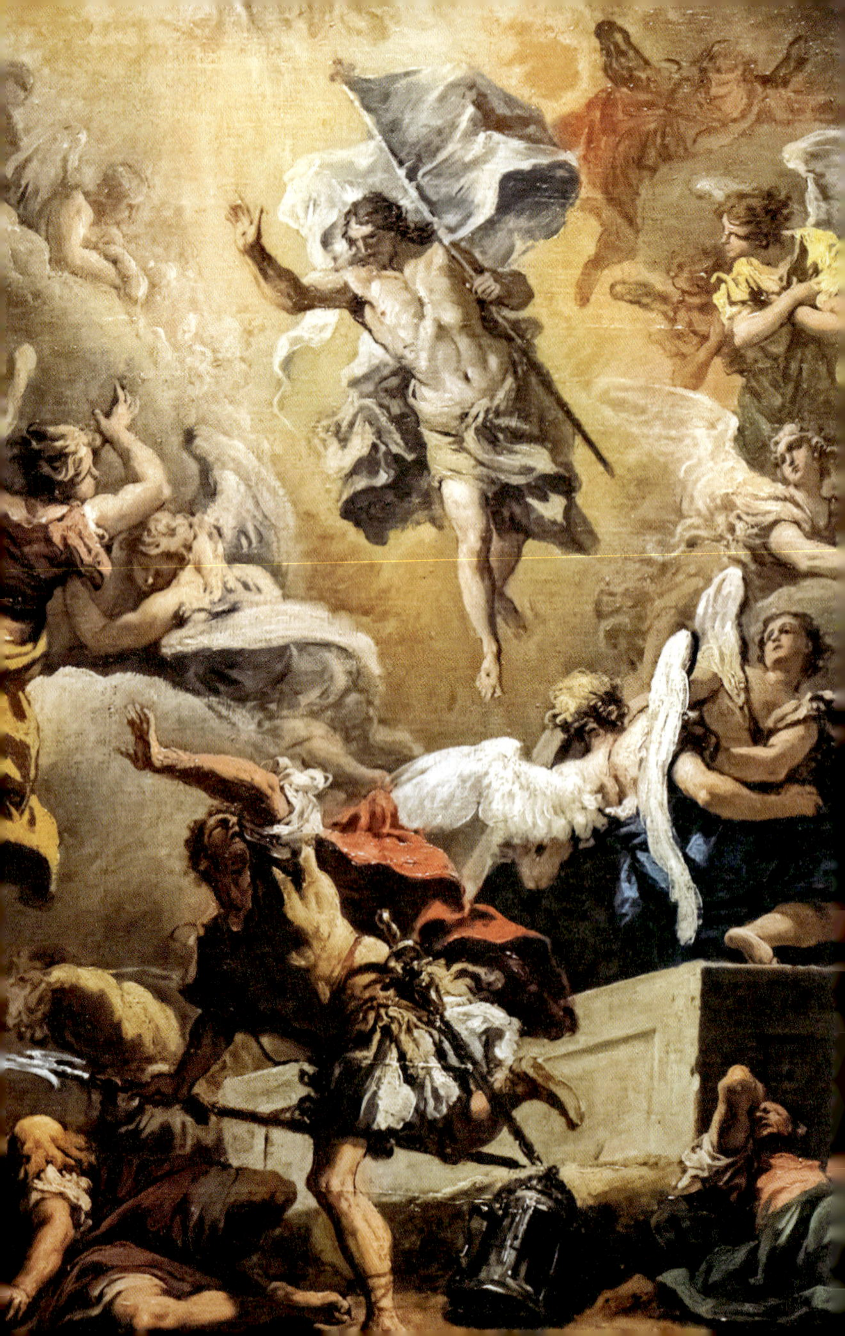

Easter

Year B

Easter Sunday, the Resurrection of the Lord

ACTS 10:34A, 37–43

PSALM 118:1–2, 16–17, 22–23

COLOSSIANS 3:1–4

JOHN 20:1–9

New Morning

The tomb was empty. In the early morning darkness of that first Easter, there was only confusion for Mary Magdalene and the other disciples. But as the daylight spread, they saw the dawning of a new creation.

At first, they didn't understand the Scripture, today's Gospel tells us. We don't know which precise Scripture texts they were supposed to understand. Perhaps it was the sign of Jonah, who rose from the belly of the great fish after three days (see Jonah 1:17). Or maybe Hosea's prophecy of Israel's restoration from exile (see Hosea 6:2). Perhaps it was the Psalmist who rejoiced that God had not abandoned him to the netherworld (see Psalm 16:9–10).

Whichever Scripture it was, as the disciples bent down into the tomb, they saw and they believed. What did they see? Burial shrouds in an empty tomb. The stone removed from the tomb. Seven times in nine verses we hear that word—"tomb."

What did they believe? That God had done what Jesus said He would do—raised Him up on the third day (see Mark 9:31; 10:34).

What they saw and believed they bore witness to, as today's First Reading tells us. Peter's speech is a summary of the Gospels from Jesus' baptism in the Jordan, to His hanging on a tree (see Deuteronomy 21:22–23), to His rising from the dead.

We are children of the Apostles, born into the new world of their witness. Our lives are now "hidden with Christ in

God," as today's Epistle says. Like them, we gather in the morning on the first day of the week. We gather to celebrate the Eucharist, the feast of the empty tomb.

We rejoice that the stones have been rolled away from our tombs, too. Each of us can shout, as we do in today's Psalm: "I shall not die, but live." They saw and believed. And we await the day they promised would come, when we, too, "will appear with Him in glory."

Jesus had to rise from the dead. Put another way, had He not risen from the dead, the sacraments wouldn't make sense. In the sacraments we encounter the living Jesus, Our Risen Lord, accepting a share of divine life, bearing truly good fruit due to the grace Jesus offers us.

> The sacraments are efficacious signs of grace, instituted by Christ and entrusted to the Church, by which divine life is dispensed to us. The visible rites by which the sacraments are celebrated signify and make present the graces proper to each sacrament. They bear fruit in those who receive them with the required dispositions. (CCC 1131)

John saw and believed. Life would be different from now on. He'd still have questions—and crosses. But the empty tomb starts John, Peter, and Mary down a new path, one leading to answers about life's ultimate meaning and purpose. It dawns on Christ's disciples, slowly at first, that the Lord Jesus is risen from the dead!

> By love, God has revealed himself and given himself to man. He has thus provided the definitive, superabundant answer to the questions that man asks himself about the meaning and purpose of his life. (CCC 68)

CHRIST, OUR PASCHAL LAMB, HAS BEEN SACRIFICED; LET US THEN FEAST WITH JOY IN THE LORD.

CF. 1 COR 5:7B–8A

What priority should the sacraments have in a Christian disciple's life, knowing that when we celebrate the sacraments we encounter the Risen Lord Jesus in unique and life-giving ways?

Who in my community of family, friends, coworkers, etc. might be struggling to find meaning and purpose in life? How might I engage in a conversation allowing me to witness to ways that my relationship with God helps make my life purposeful and full of meaning?

St. Mary Magdalene, the wonder of Christ's Resurrection defined the rest of your life. Please pray for me, that my relationship with the risen Lord will continue serving as my ultimate source of purpose and meaning throughout my earthly pilgrimage. Amen.

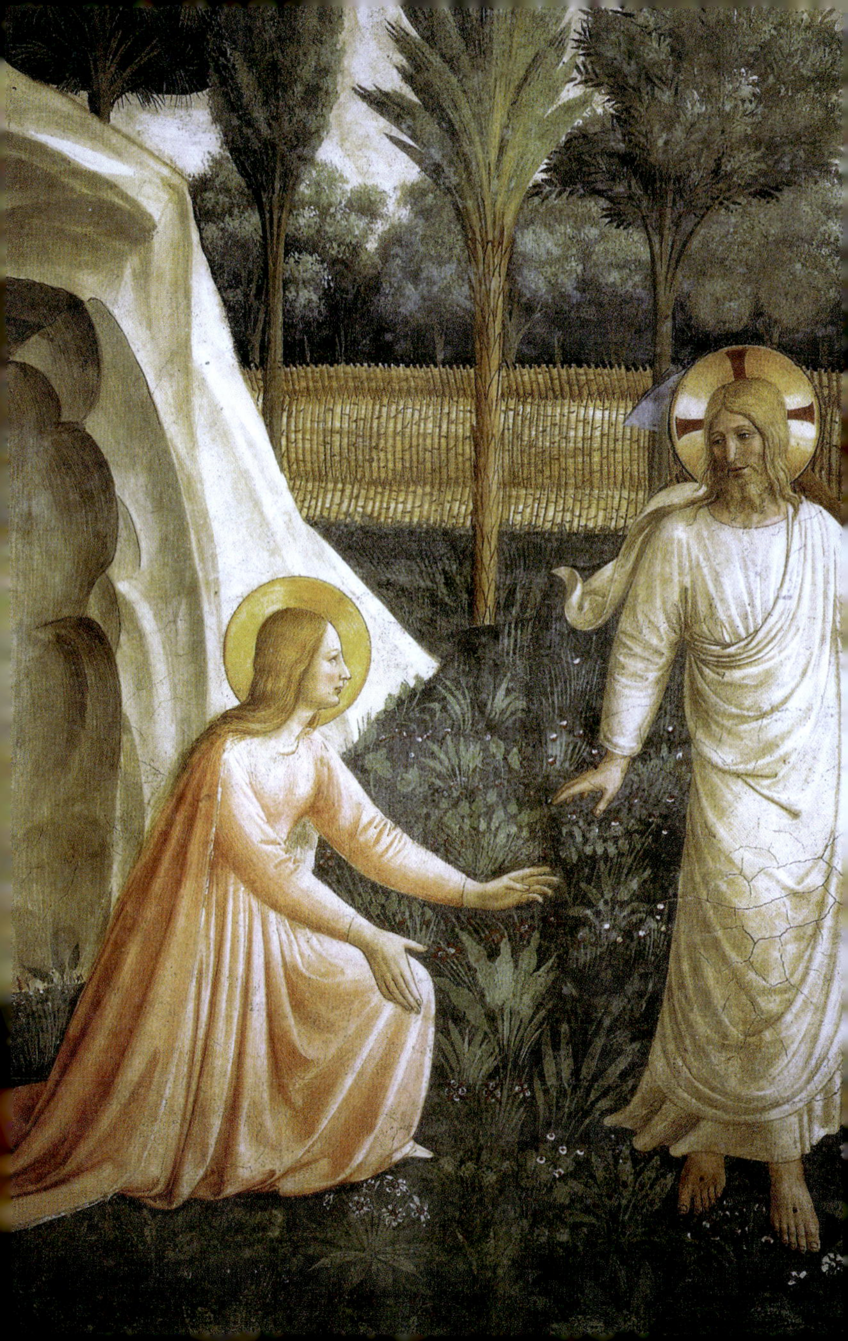

Sunday of Divine Mercy

ACTS 4:32–35

PSALM 118:2–4, 13–15, 22–24

1 JOHN 5:1–6

JOHN 20:19–31

The Day the Lord Has Made

Three times in today's Psalm we cry out a victory shout: "His mercy endures forever." Truly we've known the everlasting love of God, who has come to us as our Savior. By the blood and water that flowed from Jesus' pierced side (see John 19:34), we've been made God's children, as we hear in today's Epistle.

Yet, we've never met Jesus. We've never heard Him teach. We didn't see Him raised from the dead. His saving Word came to us in the Church—through the ministry of the Apostles, who in today's Gospel are sent as He was sent.

He was made a life-giving Spirit (see 1 Corinthians 15:45), and He filled His Apostles with that Spirit. As we hear in today's First Reading, they bore witness to His Resurrection with great power. And through their witness, handed down in the Church through the centuries, their teaching and traditions have reached us (see Acts 2:42).

We encounter Him as the Apostles did: in the breaking of the bread on the Lord's Day (see Acts 20:7; 1 Corinthians 16:2; Revelation 1:10). There is something liturgical about the way today's Gospel scenes unfold. It's as if John is trying to show us how the risen Lord comes to us in the liturgy and sacraments.

In both scenes it is Sunday night. The doors are bolted tight; yet, Jesus mysteriously comes. He greets them with an expression, "Peace be with you," used elsewhere by divine messengers (see Daniel 10:19; Judges 6:23). He shows them signs of His real bodily presence. And on both nights the disciples respond by joyfully receiving Jesus as their "Lord."

Isn't this what happens in the Mass, where Our Lord speaks to us in His Word and gives Himself to us in the sacrament of His Body and Blood? Let us approach the altar with joy, knowing that every Eucharist is the day the Lord has made, when the victory of Easter is again made wonderful in our eyes.

The Holy Spirit was given to and received by Jesus' friends and followers. This had to happen so that this infant Church could continue His mission of forgiveness and peace.

> The Holy Spirit is the protagonist, "the principal agent of the whole of the Church's mission." It is he who leads the Church on her missionary paths. "This mission continues and, in the course of history, unfolds the mission of Christ, who was sent to evangelize the poor; so the Church, urged on by the Spirit of Christ, must walk the road Christ himself walked, a way of poverty and obedience, of service and self-sacrifice even to death, a death from which he emerged victorious by his resurrection." So it is that "the blood of martyrs is the seed of Christians." (CCC 852,

quoting John Paul II, *RMiss* 21; *AG* 5; Tertullian, *Apol.* 50, 13: PL 1, 603)

Thomas' exclamation "My Lord and my God!" is one to make our own. When we address Jesus as Lord, we proclaim that, while sharing our human nature, He is at the same time, indeed, God.

> The title "Lord" indicates divine sovereignty. To confess or invoke Jesus as Lord is to believe in his divinity. "No one can say 'Jesus is Lord' except by the Holy Spirit" (*1 Cor* 12:3). (CCC 455)

How is my life different because Jesus is my Lord?

What signs do I see of the Holy Spirit's work in my community? How might I further this work?

Risen Lord Jesus, you were seen by hundreds of people after Your glorious Resurrection. Please give to all people the grace of acknowledging who You are, accepting the Divine Mercy You offer, and embracing life as Your disciple. Amen.

THOMAS, BECAUSE YOU HAVE SEEN ME, SAYS THE LORD; BLESSED ARE THOSE WHO HAVE NOT SEEN, *but* STILL BELIEVE!

JOHN 20:29

Third Sunday of Easter

ACTS 3:13–15, 17–19

PSALM 4:2, 4, 7–8, 9

1 JOHN 2:1–5A

LUKE 24:35–48

Understanding the Scriptures

In today's Gospel, Jesus teaches His Apostles how to interpret the Scriptures. He tells them that all the Scriptures of what we now call the Old Testament refer to Him. He says that all the promises found in the Old Testament have been fulfilled in His Passion, death, and Resurrection. And He tells them that these Scriptures foretell the mission of the Church: to preach forgiveness of sins to all the nations, beginning at Jerusalem.

In today's First Reading and Epistle, we see the beginnings of that mission. And we see the Apostles interpreting the Scriptures as Jesus taught them to.

God has brought to fulfillment what He announced beforehand in all the prophets, Peter preaches. His sermon is shot through with Old Testament images. He evokes Moses and the exodus, in which God revealed Himself as the ancestral God of Abraham, Isaac, and Jacob (see Exodus 3:6, 15). He identifies Jesus as Isaiah's Suffering Servant who has been glorified (see Isaiah 52:13).

John also describes Jesus in Old Testament terms. Alluding to how Israel's priests offered blood sacrifices to atone for the people's sins (see Leviticus 16; Hebrews 9–10), he says that Jesus intercedes for us before God (see Romans 8:34) and that His blood is a sacrificial expiation for the sins of the world (see 1 John 1:7).

Notice that in all three readings the Scriptures are interpreted to serve and advance the Church's mission—to reveal the truth about Jesus; to bring people to repentance, the wiping away of sins; and to lead all to the perfection of their love for God.

This is how we, too, should hear the Scriptures. Not to know more "about" Jesus but to truly know Him personally and to know His plan for our lives. In the Scriptures, the light of His face shines upon us, as we sing in today's Psalm. We know the wonders He has done throughout history. And we have the confidence to call to Him and to know that He hears and answers.

Those who had witnessed the ministry of Jesus from the very beginning had a place of honor in the very early Church. When a disciple was to be elevated to an Apostle (to replace Judas Iscariot), this witnessing was one of the criteria. A structure was evident in our Church from the earliest of days.

> Since the beginning, the ordained ministry has been conferred and exercised in three degrees: that of bishops, that of presbyters, and that of deacons. The ministries conferred by ordination are irreplaceable for the organic structure of the Church: without the bishop, presbyters, and deacons, one cannot speak of the Church (cf. St. Ignatius of Antioch, *Ad Trall.* 3, 1). (CCC 1593)

Repentance is a vital ingredient of the Good News. This repentance consists mainly of listening to the moral law and turning away from evil. The voice that beckons us toward goodness is our conscience.

> Man is obliged to follow the moral law, which urges him "to do what is good and avoid what is evil" (cf. *GS* 16). This law makes itself heard in his conscience. (CCC 1713)

How might I respond to a criticism that the Church isn't very democratic?

In what ways do I witness to my community the great deeds God has done?

St. Peter, you helped the early Church continue the mission and ministry of Jesus in accordance with His plan and promise. Pray for me as I journey through my own history, helped by the Church on my pilgrimage of repentance and reconciliation with God and neighbor. Amen.

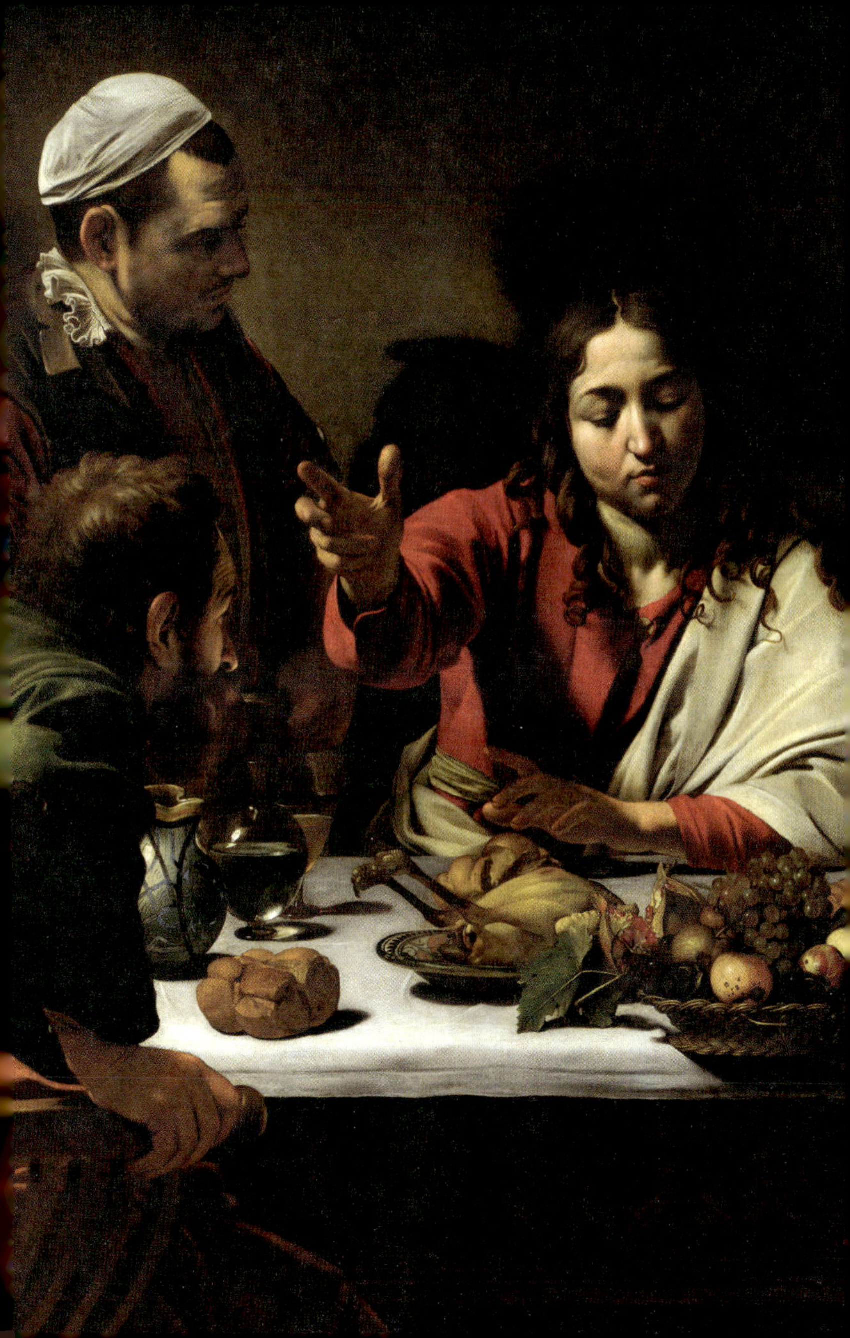

LORD JESUS,

OPEN *the* SCRIPTURES

TO US; MAKE

OUR HEARTS BURN

WHILE YOU SPEAK TO US.

CF. LUKE 24:32

Fourth Sunday of Easter

ACTS 4:8–12

PSALM 118:1, 8–9, 21–23, 26, 28, 29

1 JOHN 3:1–2

JOHN 10:11–18

The Shepherd's Voice

Jesus, in today's Gospel, says that He is the Good Shepherd the prophets had promised to Israel. He is the shepherd-prince, the new David, who frees people from bondage to sin and gathers them into one flock, the Church, under a new covenant made in His blood (see Ezekiel 34:10–13, 23–31).

His flock includes other sheep, He says, far more than the dispersed children of Israel (see Isaiah 56:8; John 11:52). And He gives His Church the mission of shepherding all peoples to the Father.

In today's First Reading, we see the beginnings of that mission in the testimony of Peter, whom the Lord appointed shepherd of His Church (see John 21:15–17). Peter tells Israel's leaders that the Psalm we sing today is a prophecy of their rejection and Crucifixion of Christ. He tells the "builders" of Israel's temple that God has made the stone they rejected the cornerstone of a new spiritual temple, the Church (see Mark 12:10–13; 1 Peter 2:4–7).

Through the ministry of the Church, the Shepherd still speaks (see Luke 10:16), forgives sins (see John 20:23), and makes His Body and Blood present, that all may know Him in the breaking of the bread (see Luke 24:35). It is a mission that will continue until all the world is one flock under the one Shepherd.

In laying down His life and taking it up again, Jesus made it possible for us to know God as He did—as sons and daughters of the Father who loves us. As we hear in today's Epistle, God calls us His children, just as He called Israel His son when He led them out of Egypt and made His covenant with them (see Exodus 4:22–23; Revelation 21:7).

Today, let us listen for His voice as He speaks to us in the Scriptures, and vow again to be more faithful followers. And let us give thanks for the blessings He bestows from His altar.

To serve the way Jesus serves is a unique calling. Certainly, all Christians are called to participate in Jesus' ministry through a variety of means. Yet, in order to serve the entire community, God calls specific men to participate in the life of the community in the person of the God-Man, Jesus, as well as in His name. Thus, the ordained, ministerial priesthood complements the way all of the baptized share in Jesus' priestly ministry.

> The whole Church is a priestly people. Through Baptism all the faithful share in the priesthood of Christ. This participation is called the "common priesthood of the faithful." Based on this common priesthood and ordered to its service, there exists another participation in the mission of Christ: the ministry conferred by the sacrament of Holy Orders, where the task is to serve in the name

> and in the person of Christ the Head in the midst of the community. (CCC 1591)

Who are these other sheep that do not belong to the fold? Whoever they are, in God's eyes there will eventually be one shepherd leading one flock; the key is to listen for the voice of Jesus, allowing Him to lead.

The closest earthly image to the united flock that Our Father desires is the Church led by Christ's vicar, the bishop of Rome. Bits and pieces of the fullness of truth can be found outside the visible structure of Catholicism, though; it can be helpful when interacting with people of various faiths to keep this in mind.

> "The sole Church of Christ which in the Creed we profess to be one, holy, catholic, and apostolic, . . . subsists in the Catholic Church, which is governed by the successor of Peter and by the bishops in communion with him. Nevertheless, many elements of sanctification and of truth are found outside its visible confines" (*LG* 8). (CCC 870)

> **I AM THE GOOD SHEPHERD,**
> **SAYS THE LORD;**
> **I KNOW MY SHEEP,**
> **AND MINE KNOW ME.**
>
> JOHN 10:14

How might I explain the similarities and differences between an ordained priest and the rest of the baptized?

How can I deepen my interaction with people of other faiths without taking anything away from my own Catholic faith and practice?

Jesus, You are the Good Shepherd. Help me, please, to hear Your voice when the shepherds you've appointed—bishops and pastors, especially—call me to love all my neighbors as You have loved me. Amen.

Fifth Sunday of Easter

ACTS 9:26–31

PSALM 22:26–27, 28, 30, 31–32

1 JOHN 3:18–24

JOHN 15:1–8

On the Vine

In today's Gospel, Jesus tells us that He is the true vine that God intended Israel to be—the source of divine life and wisdom for the nations (see Sirach 24:17–24). In Baptism, each of us was joined to Him by the Holy Spirit. As a branch grows from a tree, our souls are to draw life from Him, nourished by His Word and the Eucharist.

Paul in today's First Reading seeks to be grafted onto the visible expression of Christ the true vine—His Church. Once the chief persecutor of the Church, he encounters initial resistance and suspicion. But he is known by his fruits, by his powerful witness to the Lord working in his life (see Matthew 7:16–20).

We, too, are commanded today to bear good fruits as His disciples, so that our lives give glory to God. Like Paul's life, our lives must bear witness to His goodness.

Jesus cautions us, however, that if we're bearing fruit, we can expect that God will "prune" us like a gardener trimming and cutting back a plant so that it will grow stronger and bear even more fruit. He is teaching us today how to look at our sufferings and trials with the eyes of faith. We need to see our struggles as pruning, by which we are being disciplined and trained so that we can grow in holiness and bear fruits of righteousness (see Hebrews 12:4–11).

We need to always remain rooted in Him, as today's Epistle tells us. We remain in Him by keeping His commandment of love; by pondering His words, letting them dwell richly in us (see Colossians 3:16); and by always seeking to do what pleases Him. In everything we must be guided by humility, remembering that, apart from Him, we can do nothing.

As we sing in today's Psalm, we must fulfill our vows, turning to the Lord in worship, proclaiming his praises, until all families come to know His justice in their lives.

Being thrown into a fire and burned brings to mind thoughts of hell. But what is hell really like? Because we are made to be united with God, hell is that place where we are cut off from God—forever. More than any physical pain, the torment of estrangement from the source of our happiness would be a hopelessly agonizing punishment.

> Hell's principal punishment consists of eternal separation from God in whom alone man can have the life and happiness for which he was created and for which he longs. (CCC 1057)

How do we remain in Jesus, and He in us? There are many ways, and prominent among them is prayer. When we pray, we follow Jesus' example and enjoy the relationship that He has with Our Father. Filled with the Holy Spirit, we can, like Jesus, ask God to help us bear fruit as disciples of His only Son. And the words of the Son will remain in us.

"Prayer is the raising of one's mind and heart to God or the requesting of good things from God" (St. John Damascene, *De fide orth.* 3, 24: PG 94, 1089C). (CCC 2590)

REMAIN IN ME AS I REMAIN IN YOU, SAYS THE LORD. WHOEVER REMAINS IN ME WILL BEAR MUCH FRUIT.

JOHN 15:4A, 5B

Along with the vine and branch analogy, what other comparisons can I think of that convey the relationship between Jesus and me?

For whom in my community can I, right now, request good things from God?

Heavenly Father, the reality of hell is frightening. Please help me to remain close to You, Jesus, and the Holy Spirit so my decisions are motivated by love more than fear. May my life bear truly good fruit by Your grace and mercy. Amen.

Sixth Sunday of Easter

ACTS 10:25–26, 34–35, 44–48

PSALM 98:1, 2–3, 3–4

1 JOHN 4:7–10

JOHN 15:9–17

Begotten by Love

"God is love," and He revealed that love in sending His only Son to be a sacrificial offering for our sins. In these words from today's Epistle, we should hear an echo of the story of Abraham's offering of Isaac at the dawn of salvation history. Because Abraham obeyed God's command and did not withhold his only beloved son, God promised that Abraham's descendants, the children of Israel, would be the source of blessing for all nations (see Genesis 22:16–18).

We see that promise coming to fulfillment in today's First Reading. God pours out His Spirit upon the Gentiles, the non-Israelites, as they listen to Peter's preaching. Notice they receive the same gifts received by the devout Jews who heard Peter's preaching at Pentecost—the Spirit comes to rest upon them and they speak in tongues, glorifying God (see Acts 2:5–11).

In His love today, God reveals that His salvation embraces both the house of Israel and peoples of all nations. Not by circumcision or blood relation to Abraham but by faith in the Word of Christ, sealed in the Sacrament of Baptism, all peoples are to be made children of Abraham, heirs to God's covenants of promise (see Galatians 3:7–9; Ephesians 2:12).

This is the wondrous work of God that we sing of in today's Psalm. It is the work of the Church, the good fruit for which Jesus chooses and appoints His Apostles in today's Gospel. As Peter raises up Cornelius today, the Church continues to lift all eyes to Christ, the only one in whose name they can find salvation.

In the Church, each of us has been begotten by the love of God. But the Scriptures today reveal that this divine gift brings with it a command and a duty. We are to love one another as we have been loved. We are to lay down our lives in giving ourselves to others, that they, too, might find friendship with Christ and new life through Him.

God initiates love; He makes the first move. The Father inspires virtues. We respond to this inspiration to our immeasurable benefit: we enjoy the life of Father, Son, and Holy Spirit.

> The theological virtues [of faith, hope, and love] dispose Christians to live in a relationship with the Holy Trinity. They have God for their origin, their motive, and their object—God known by faith, God hoped in and loved for his own sake. (CCC 1840)

Jesus reveals the greatest expression of love. His teaching had been hinted at for centuries, especially in the Ten Commandments, or Decalogue. Everything Jesus heard from His Father culminates in His command and example of love.

The Old Law is the first stage of revealed law. Its moral prescriptions are summed up in the Ten Commandments. (CCC 1980)

WHOEVER LOVES ME WILL KEEP MY WORD, SAYS THE LORD, AND MY FATHER WILL LOVE HIM AND WE WILL COME TO HIM.

JOHN 14:23

With which of the three theological virtues does God seem to have blessed me most? For which of the three do I need to pray with a special intensity?

Who in your community do you find it difficult to love as Jesus loves this person? Ask Our Father in Jesus' name to help you love all people as Jesus does.

Eternal God—Father, Son, and Holy Spirit—You invite me to participate in the loving communion that flourishes between You as the Most Holy Trinity. I thank You for befriending me during my earthly life and offering me eternal joy with You in heaven. Amen.

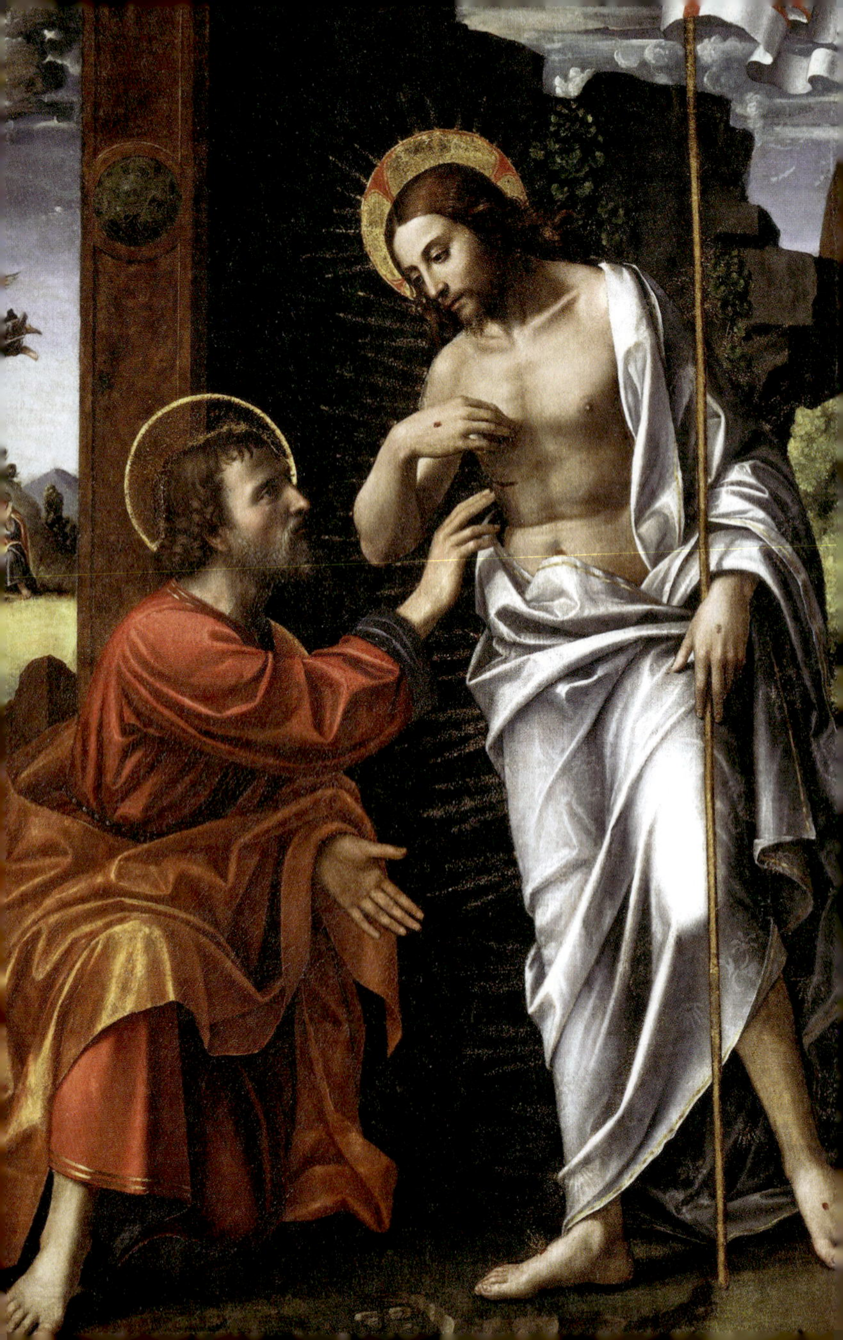

Seventh Sunday of Easter

ACTS 1:15–17, 20A, 20C–26

PSALM 103:1–2, 11–12, 19–20

1 JOHN 4:11–16

JOHN 17:11B–19

The Kingdom Remains

Today's First Reading begins by giving us a time frame—the events we hear about take place during the days between Christ's Ascension and Pentecost. We're at the same point in our liturgical year. On Thursday, we celebrated His being taken up in glory; and next Sunday, we will celebrate His sending of the Spirit upon the Church.

Jesus' prayer in the Gospel today also captures a mood of departure and anticipation. He is telling us today how it will be when He is no longer in the world. By His Ascension, the Lord has established His throne in heaven, as we sing in today's Psalm. His kingdom is His Church, which continues His mission on earth.

Jesus fashioned His kingdom as a new Jerusalem and a new house of David (see Psalm 122:3–5; Revelation 21:9–14). He entrusted this kingdom to His Twelve Apostles, who were to preside at the Eucharistic table and rule with Him over the restored twelve tribes of Israel (see Luke 22:29–30). The Twelve Apostles symbolize the twelve tribes and hence the fulfillment of God's plan for Israel (see Galatians 6:16). That's why it was crucial to replace Judas—so that the Church in its fullness receives the Spirit at Pentecost.

Peter's leadership of the Apostles is another key element of the Church as it is depicted today. Notice that Peter is unquestionably in control, interpreting the Scriptures, deciding a course of action, even defining the nature of the apostolic ministry.

No one has ever seen God, as we hear in today's Epistle. Yet, through the Church founded on His Apostles, the witnesses to the Resurrection, the world will come to know and believe in God's love, that He sent His Son to be our Savior.

Through the Church, Jesus' pledge still comes to us: if we love, God will remain with us in our trials and protect us from the evil one. By His Word of truth He will help us grow in holiness, the perfection of love.

Jesus clearly desires that His followers be united. For this reason, we know that a clear sign or mark of the Church established by Jesus is that she is united. The Church is one.

> The Church is one: she acknowledges one Lord, confesses one faith, is born of one Baptism, forms only one Body, is given life by the one Spirit, for the sake of one hope (cf. *Eph* 4:3–5), at whose fulfillment all divisions will be overcome. (CCC 866)

Unity, or oneness, transcends in some ways the Church's visible membership. More and more, unity among human persons has visible international or global dimensions. Because all humans share a bond through their Creator, it is fitting that efforts to build community at the international level are underway.

> It is the role of the state to defend and promote the common good of civil society. The common good of the whole human family calls for an organization of society on the international level. (CCC 1927)

How is my level of oneness with the people with whom I most need to be united (for example, my spouse)? What might I do to enhance the degree of this unity?

What are some ways I can be an agent of unity—a peacemaker, even—within my community?

Holy Spirit, You show me love, truth, and unity. Help me retain the hope felt when renewing my baptismal promises: "This is our faith. This is the faith of the Church. We are proud to profess it in Christ Jesus our Lord." Amen.

I WILL NOT LEAVE

YOU ORPHANS,

SAYS *the* LORD.

I WILL COME BACK TO YOU,

AND YOUR HEARTS

WILL REJOICE.

CF. JOHN 14:18

Solemnity of the Ascension of the Lord

ACTS 1:1–11

PSALM 47:2–3, 6–7, 8–9

EPHESIANS 1:17–23 (OR 4:1–13; OR 4:1–7, 11–13)

MARK 16:15–20

More to the Story

In today's First Reading, St. Luke gives the surprising news that there is more of the story to be told. It did not end with the empty tomb or with Jesus' appearances to the Apostles over the course of forty days. Jesus' saving work will have a liturgical consummation. He is the great high priest, and He has still to ascend to the heavenly Jerusalem, there to celebrate the feast in the true Holy of Holies.

The truth of this feast shines forth from the Letter to the Hebrews, where we read of the great high priest's passing through the heavens, the sinless intercessor's sacrifice on our behalf (see Hebrews 4:14–15).

Indeed, His intercession will lead to the Holy Spirit's descent in fire upon the Church. Luke spells out that promise in the First Reading for the feast of the Ascension: "in a few days you will be baptized with the Holy Spirit" (Acts 1:5). The Ascension is the preliminary feast that directs the Church's attention forward to Pentecost. On that day, salvation will be complete; for salvation is not simply expiation for sins (that would be wonder enough), but it is something even greater than that. Expiation is itself a necessary precondition of our adoption as God's children. To live that divine life, we must receive the Holy Spirit. To receive the Holy Spirit, we must be purified through Baptism.

The Responsorial Psalm presents the Ascension in terms familiar from the worship of the Jerusalem temple in the days of King Solomon: "God mounts his throne to shouts of joy: a blare of trumpets for the Lord" (Psalm 47). The priest-king takes his place at the head of the people, ruling over the nations, establishing peace.

The Epistle strikes a distinctively Paschal note. In the early Church, as today, Easter was the normal time for the baptism of adult converts. The sacrament was often called "illumination" or "enlightenment" (see, for example, Hebrews 10:32) because of the light that came with God's saving grace. St. Paul, in his letter to the Ephesians, speaks in terms of glory that leads to greater glories still, as Ascension leads to Pentecost: "May the eyes of your hearts be enlightened," he writes, as he looks to the divinization of the believers. Their "hope" is "his inheritance among the holy ones," the saints who have been adopted into God's family and now rule with him at the Father's right hand.

This is the "Good News" the Apostles are commissioned to spread—to the whole world, to all nations, beginning from Jerusalem—at the first Ascension. It's the Good News we must spread today.

"Whoever believes and is baptized will be saved" (Mark 16:16). Baptism is profoundly important. Being baptized helps us avoid being eternally deprived of God's presence in heaven.

> Adam and Eve transmitted to their descendants human nature wounded by their own first sin and hence deprived of original holiness and justice; this deprivation is called "original sin." (CCC 417)

For most of us, our vocation doesn't include driving out demons, picking up serpents, and drinking deadly things. God's grace, though, makes all things possible in accordance with His holy and perfect will. Whatever work God gives you to do, know that He works in you—that the Lord works with you—by His grace and mercy.

> Grace is the help God gives us to respond to our vocation of becoming his adopted sons. It introduces us into the intimacy of the Trinitarian life. (CCC 2021)

GO AND TEACH ALL NATIONS,
SAYS THE LORD;
I AM WITH YOU ALWAYS,
UNTIL THE END OF THE WORLD.

MATTHEW 28:19A, 20B

How is my life different due to the Sacrament of Baptism? What signs of God working in and with me might I acknowledge today?

Does everyone in my life know what Baptism is, why it's so important, and that they're invited to pursue being baptized—or to live out their baptism more intentionally, joyfully, and fruitfully?

Jesus, as You were ascending to the Father You made clear how important Baptism is. Please work in and through me so that everyone I meet knows what Baptism is, why it matters, and that they are invited to pursue being baptized or living out their baptismal promises more fully. Amen.

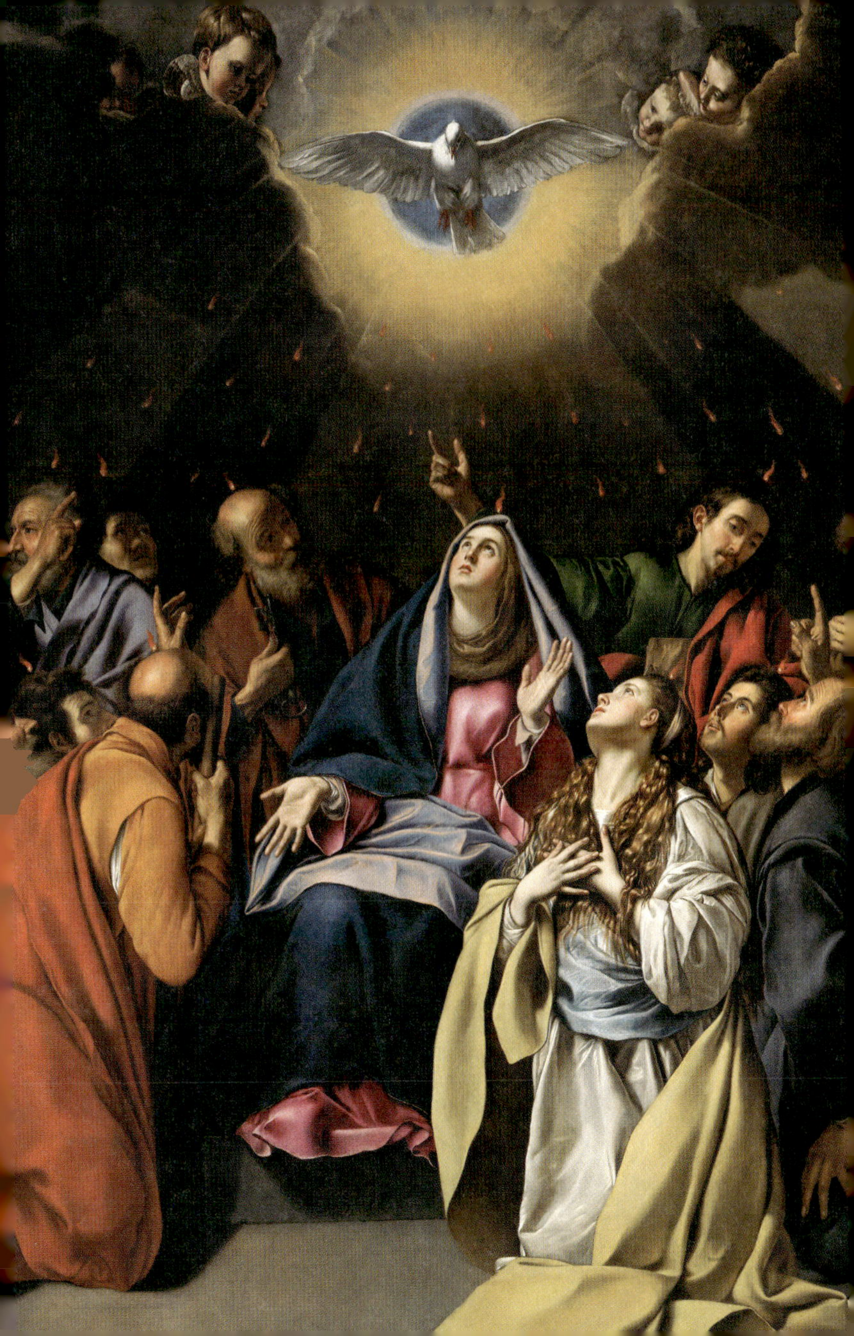

COME, HOLY SPIRIT,

FILL THE HEARTS

OF YOUR FAITHFUL

AND KINDLE IN THEM

THE FIRE *of* YOUR LOVE.

SEQUENCE FOR PENTECOST

Pentecost

ACTS 2:1–11

PSALM 104:1, 24, 29–31, 34

1 CORINTHIANS 12:3B–7, 12–13

JOHN 20:19–23

A New Wind

The giving of the Spirit to the new people of God crowns the mighty acts of the Father in salvation history.

The Jewish feast of Pentecost called all devout Jews to Jerusalem to celebrate their birth as God's chosen people in the covenant law given to Moses at Sinai (see Leviticus 23:15–21; Deuteronomy 16:9–11). In today's First Reading, the mysteries prefigured in that feast are fulfilled in the pouring out of the Spirit on Mary and the Apostles (see Acts 1:14).

The Spirit seals the new law and new covenant brought by Jesus, written not on stone tablets but on the hearts of believers, as the prophets promised (see Jeremiah 31:31–34; 2 Corinthians 3:2–8; Romans 8:2).

The Spirit is revealed as the life-giving breath of the Father, the Wisdom by which He made all things, as we sing in today's Psalm. In the beginning, the Spirit came as a "mighty wind" sweeping over the face of the earth (see Genesis 1:2). In the new creation of Pentecost, the Spirit again comes as "a strong, driving wind" to renew the face of the earth.

As God fashioned the first man out of dust and filled him with His Spirit (see Genesis 2:7), in today's Gospel we see the New Adam become a life-giving Spirit, breathing new life into the Apostles (see 1 Corinthians 15:45, 47).

Like a river of living water, for all ages He will pour out His Spirit on His Body, the Church, as we hear in today's Epistle (see also John 7:37–39).

We receive that Spirit in the sacraments, being made a "new creation" in Baptism (see 2 Corinthians 5:17; Galatians 6:15).

Drinking of the one Spirit in the Eucharist (see 1 Corinthians 10:4), we are the firstfruits of a new humanity—fashioned from out of every nation under heaven, with no distinctions of wealth or language or race, a people born of the Spirit.

The Holy Spirit is crucially important in interpreting the Bible. In many cases, there are true interpretations of Scripture and those that are simply inaccurate. The Spirit, working in the magisterium, or teaching authority of our Church, helps us understand and apply what's in the Bible to our everyday life.

> Interpretation of the inspired Scripture must be attentive above all to what God wants to reveal through the sacred authors for our salvation. What comes from the Spirit is not fully "understood except by the Spirit's action" (cf. Origen, *Hom. in Ex.* 4, 5: PG 12, 320). (CCC 137)

When the Spirit guides you to all truth, He may occasionally steer you away from television, the internet, etc., which doesn't always offer the clear truth. In seeking the truth, we must be mindful that not all media programming puts priority on justice, truth, and freedom. We need prudence and other virtues to be wise consumers of media.

> Society has a right to information based on truth, freedom, and justice. One should practice moderation and discipline in the use of the social communications media. (CCC 2512)

What degree of moderation and discipline do I practice in using social communications media?

How involved am I in a good, Catholic Bible study group? Might I increase my involvement—or begin it?

SS. Peter and Andrew, James and John, Philip and Bartholomew, Thomas and Matthew, James, Thaddeus, and Simon, as the Holy Spirit descended on you and the Blessed Virgin Mary at Pentecost, please pray that I will use the Holy Spirit's gifts to help bear truly good fruit by God's grace and mercy. Amen.

Ordinary Time

Year B

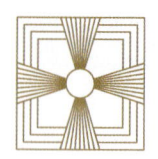

Solemnity of the Holy Trinity

DEUTERONOMY 4:32–34, 39–40
PSALM 33:4–5, 6, 9, 18–19, 20, 22
ROMANS 8:14–17
MATTHEW 28:16–20

Family of Love

Last Sunday, we celebrated the sending of the Spirit, which sealed God's new covenant and made a new creation. In this new creation, we live in the family of God, who has revealed Himself as a Trinity of love. We share in His divine nature through His Body and Blood (see 2 Peter 1:4). This is the meaning of the three feasts that cap the Easter season: Pentecost, Trinity Sunday, and Corpus Christi.

These feasts should be intimate reminders of how deeply God loves us, how He chose us from before the foundation of the world to be His children (see Ephesians 1:4–5).

Today's readings illuminate how all God's words and works were meant to prepare for the revelation of the Trinity and God's blessing in Jesus Christ—the blessing we inherited in Baptism and renew in each Eucharist.

By God's Word the heavens and earth were filled with His kindness, we sing in today's Psalm. Out of love, God called Abraham and chose his descendants to be His own people, Moses says in today's First Reading (see Deuteronomy 4:20, 37). Through the Israelites, God revealed to the nations that He alone is Lord, and there is no other.

In Jesus, God's Word took flesh as a son of Abraham (see Matthew 1:1). And Jesus reveals in the Gospel today that the one God is Father, Son, and Spirit, and that He desires to make all peoples His own.

As He led Israel out of Egypt, God freed us from slavery, Paul says in today's Epistle. As He adopted Israel (see Romans

9:4), He gives us the Spirit by which we can know Him as Our Father.

As God's heirs, we receive the commissions of both Moses and Jesus today. We are to fix our hearts on Christ and to observe all that He has commanded. The Eucharist is His pledge that He will be with us until the end, that He will deliver us from death to live forever in the promised land of His kingdom.

Jesus continues to command action through His teaching voice, the Church. Our Church offers a few practical guidelines, or precepts, to help us express our faith concretely day in and day out. When we do so, we become better disciples and by our example help make disciples of all the nations.

> The first precept ("You shall attend Mass on Sundays and on holy days of obligation and rest from servile labor") requires the faithful to sanctify the day commemorating the Resurrection of the Lord as well as the principle liturgical feasts honoring the mysteries of the Lord, the Blessed Virgin Mary, and the saints; in the first place, by participating in the Eucharistic celebration, in which the Christian community is gathered,

and by resting from those works and activities which could impede such a sanctification of these days.

The second precept ("You shall confess your sins at least once a year") ensures preparation for the Eucharist by the reception of the sacrament of reconciliation, which continues Baptism's work of conversion and forgiveness.

The third precept ("You shall receive the sacrament of the Eucharist at least during the Easter season") guarantees as a minimum the reception of the Lord's Body and Blood in connection with the Paschal feasts, the origin and center of the Christian liturgy.

The fourth precept ("You shall observe the days of fasting and abstinence established by the Church") ensures the times of ascesis and penance which prepare us for the liturgical feasts and help us acquire mastery over our instincts and freedom of heart.

The fifth precept ("You shall help to provide for the needs of the Church") means that the faithful are obliged to assist with the material needs of the Church, each according to his own ability.

The faithful also have the duty of providing for the material needs of the Church, each according to his own abilities. (CCC 2042, 2043)

GLORY TO THE FATHER, THE SON, AND THE HOLY SPIRIT; TO GOD WHO IS, WHO WAS, AND WHO IS TO COME

REVELATION 1:8

Do I have an occasional doubt or two about some aspect of the faith? (If so, recall that even the Eleven doubted; but they obeyed, took action, and persevered to glory.)

Holy days of obligation are to be treated as if they are a Sunday. Would I consider witnessing to my coworkers the importance of the Church in my life by taking holy days of obligation off work as a personal or vacation day?

Holy Trinity—Father, Son, and Holy Spirit—thank You for loving me and inviting me to know Your kindness. May my life reflect authentic kindness to each person I encounter. Amen.

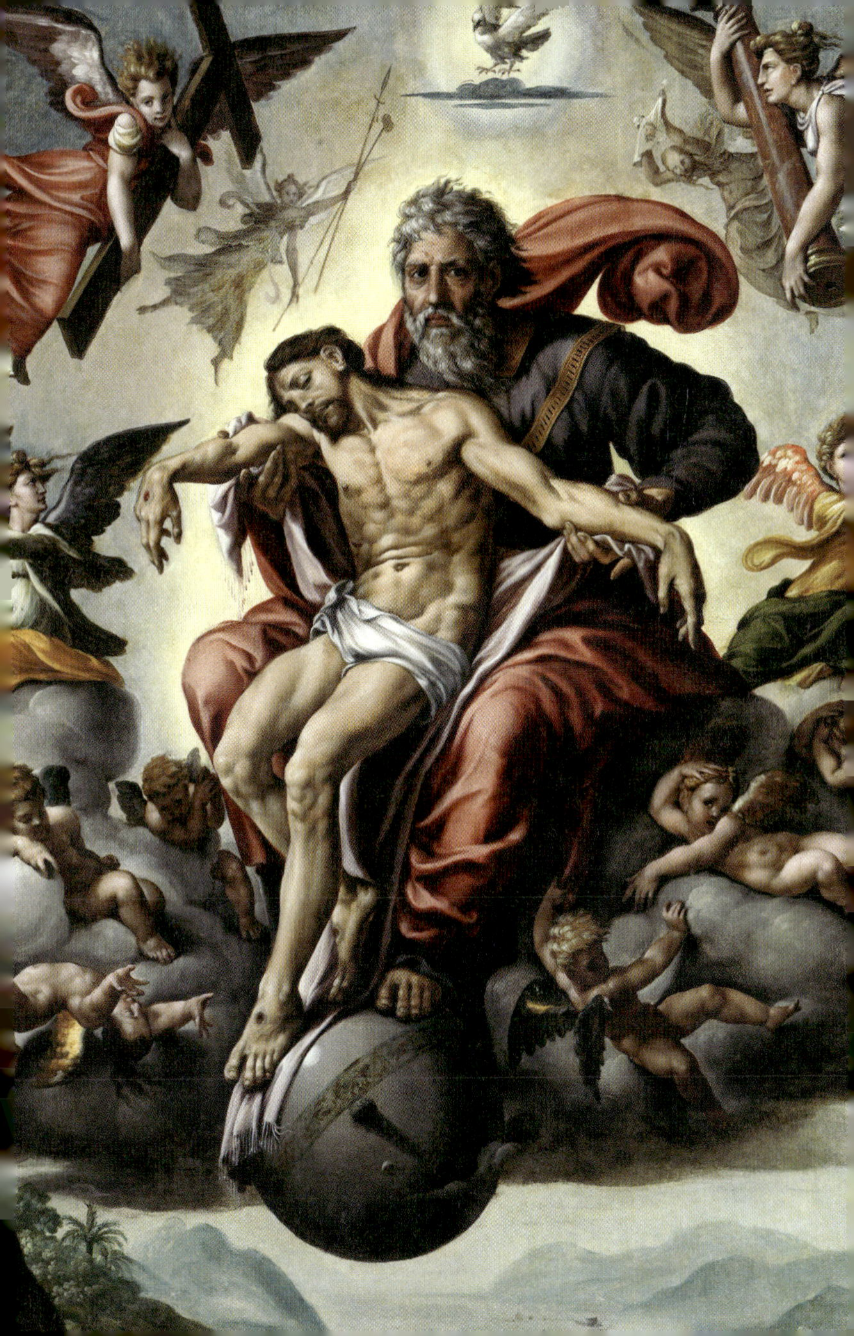

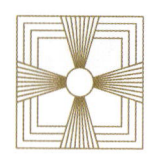

Solemnity of the Most Holy Body and Blood of Christ

EXODUS 24:3–8

PSALM 116:12–13, 15–16, 17–18

HEBREWS 9:11–15

MARK 14:12–16, 22–26

Blood of the Covenant

All of today's readings are set in the context of the Passover. The First Reading recalls the old covenant celebrated at Sinai following the first Passover and the exodus. In sprinkling the blood of the covenant on the Israelites, Moses was symbolizing God's desire in this covenant to make them His family, His "blood" relations.

Quoting Moses' words in today's Gospel, Jesus elevates and transforms this covenant symbol to an extraordinary reality. In the new covenant made in the blood of Christ, we truly become one with His Body and Blood.

The first covenant made with Moses and Israel at Sinai was but a shadow of this new and greater covenant made by Christ with all humankind in that upper room (see Hebrews 10:1). The Passover that Jesus celebrates with His Twelve Apostles "actualizes," makes real, what could only be symbolized by Moses' sacrifice at the altar with twelve pillars. What Jesus does today is establish His Church as the new Israel and His Eucharist as the new worship of the living God.

In offering Himself to God through the Spirit, Jesus delivered Israel from the transgressions of the first covenant. And, as we hear in today's Epistle, by His blood He purified us and made us capable of true worship.

God does not want dead works or animal sacrifices. He wants our own flesh and blood, our own lives, consecrated to Him, offered as a living sacrifice. This is the sacrifice of praise and thanksgiving that we sing of in today's Psalm. This is the Eucharist.

What we do in memory of Him is to pledge our lives to Him, to renew our promise to live by the words of His covenant and to be His servants. There is no other return we can offer to Him for the eternal inheritance He has won for us. So let us approach the altar, calling upon His name in thanksgiving, taking up the cup of salvation.

The Passover celebrates God keeping His promise, His covenant, with Abraham. Through Moses, God delivers His people from the slavery of Egypt. Through Jesus' sacrifice, our heavenly Father delivers us from the slavery of sin and death.

> God chose Abraham and made a covenant with him and his descendants. By the covenant God formed his people and revealed his law to them through Moses. Through the prophets, he prepared them to accept the salvation destined for all humanity. (CCC 72)

It was bread that Jesus took, blessed, broke, and gave. Wine as well. And priests to this day take bread, bless it, break it, and give it to us. This is our saving feast of passing over from death and sin to new life in Jesus.

The essential signs of the Eucharistic sacrament are wheat bread and grape wine, on which the blessing of the Holy Spirit is invoked and the priest pronounces the words of consecration spoken by Jesus during the Last Supper: "This is my body which will be given up for you. . . . This is the cup of my blood. . . ." (CCC 1412)

How am I at keeping my promises? What might I do to improve in this regard?

When a promise is broken, it affects not just one person but those around them. In what ways have broken or kept promises impacted my community?

St. Mark, the early Christians to whom you addressed your Gospel celebrated and cherished the Most Holy Eucharist. Pray for me, that I acknowledge the Real Presence of Jesus in the Blessed Sacrament, allowing His grace to form me and my parish community as members of the Body of Christ. Amen.

I AM THE LIVING BREAD

THAT CAME DOWN

from HEAVEN,

SAYS THE LORD;

WHOEVER EATS THIS BREAD

WILL LIVE FOREVER.

JOHN 6:51

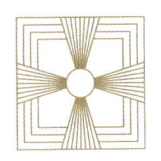

Ninth Sunday in Ordinary Time

DEUTERONOMY 5:12–15

PSALM 81:3–4, 5–6, 7–8, 10–11

2 CORINTHIANS 4:6–11

MARK 2:23–3:6 OR 2:23–28

The Lord of the Sabbath

Today's readings give us the rest of the story in the story of our rest.

In a key passage from Deuteronomy, we hear God's commandment to remember the Sabbath and keep it holy. This is the longest of the Ten Commandments. The Lord makes it clear that everyone should enjoy a day of leisure and worship. The Chosen People are to provide the opportunity not just for themselves but also for their employees and slaves, for foreigners living in their land, and even for livestock!

Psalm 81 celebrates the fact that God legislated leisure as a non-negotiable part of life on the Sabbath and at all solemn feasts. God's people are to be unburdened—and they are to relieve others of their burdens.

St. Paul understood the spirit of this law. He saw that, in the fullness of time, Christians would observe a perpetual feast, marked by joy and charity, manifesting the life of Jesus in their own lives.

For Jesus has revealed the full meaning of the Sabbath. In the Gospel, St. Mark presents Jesus' teaching in stark contrast to that of the Pharisees. The Pharisees use the commandment as a pretext for persecuting Him. In the Scripture immediately following today's Gospel, Jesus works miracles on the Sabbath, and the Pharisees insist that He violates the law by doing so. He asks them: "Is it lawful to do good on the sabbath rather than to do evil, to save life rather than to destroy it?"

Well, it's *never* lawful to do evil or commit murder—not on the Sabbath or any day. But Jesus knows the hearts of these men, as we see at the end when they go out immediately and plot to kill Him.

The Sabbath commandment is largely ignored in our time. But it was honored by Moses, David, Paul, and Jesus. May our Sundays be like theirs: filled with joy, charity, and right worship.

The Sabbath was made for man. Sometimes people think they can get ahead by doing extra things on Sunday. Extra work. Extra shopping. Sometimes they'll even sacrifice going to Mass to get these things done—to get ahead.

When we fail to observe the Lord's Day, we hurt ourselves. God gives us Sunday as a gift. God made Sunday for you.

> On Sundays and other holy days of obligation the faithful are bound . . . to abstain from those labors and business concerns which impede the worship to be rendered to God, the joy which is proper to the Lord's Day, or the proper relaxation of mind and body. (CCC 2193)

David's deeds say a lot in this instance. Jesus' words in turn reveal true teaching from God Himself. God, out of love, chose to start revealing Himself to human persons. He did so to and through David. He does so in the teaching, action, and Person of Jesus.

God has revealed himself to man by gradually communicating his own mystery in deeds and in words. (CCC 69)

YOUR WORD, O LORD, IS TRUTH; CONSECRATE US IN THE TRUTH.

CF. JOHN 17:17B, 17A

Jesus uses an example from Scripture to make a point. How often do I do this? How might I familiarize myself with the Bible more deeply so as to be more like Jesus in this regard?

In what ways do I see God acting within my communities? How might I help make His presence more noticeable?

Holy Spirit, please renew my appreciation of Sunday as the Lord's Day. Help me embrace the gift of the Sabbath by worshipping God, accepting His joy, and prioritizing the refreshment of mind and body that Jesus encourages me to pursue to the best of my ability. Amen.

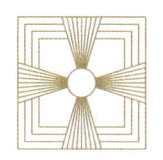

Tenth Sunday in Ordinary Time

GENESIS 3:9–15

PSALM 130:1–2, 3–4, 5–6, 7–8

2 CORINTHIANS 4:13–5:1

MARK 3:20–35

The Promised One

In today's Gospel, Jesus has just been healing and casting out demons in Galilee. Along with the crowds, who flock to Him so that He can't even take a break to eat, come people who do not understand what He is doing. Even His friends think He has lost His mind and needs to be taken away for a while. But the scribes who came down from Jerusalem are not just honestly mistaken; they accuse Him of being possessed by the prince of demons.

The reality is just the opposite. Jesus is revealing Himself as the one promised in our First Reading. He is the seed of the woman who has come to crush the head of the demonic serpent. In the parable of the Strong Man, Jesus reveals that He has come not just to punish the devil but to free those bound by him. As St. Bede explains, "The Lord has also bound the strong man, that is, the devil: which means, He has restrained him from seducing the elect, and entering into his house, the world; He has spoiled his house, and His goods, that is men, because He has snatched them from the snares of the devil, and has united them to His Church."

The scribes blaspheme by attributing this work of the Holy Spirit to demons. Jesus adds a statement that shocks us at first: "Whoever blasphemes against the Holy Spirit never has forgiveness." That does not mean that there are any limits to the mercy of God (see CCC 1864). Rather, the only sin that cannot be forgiven is the deliberate refusal to accept the mercy offered through the Holy Spirit. We must imitate those who sat at Jesus' feet. For, as He said, "Whoever does the will of God is my brother, and sister, and mother."

The Father, the Son, and the Holy Spirit desire us to be in communion with them. United with the Blessed Trinity, no power can ultimately harm us. Our Church is an entirely unique place and way to encounter the Triune God, learning and doing His will.

> The Holy Spirit, whom Christ the head pours out on his members, builds, animates, and sanctifies the Church. She is the sacrament of the Holy Trinity's communion with men. (CCC 747)

Jesus makes it abundantly clear: doing the will of God is profoundly important if we desire closeness with Him. Moral teachings like the Ten Commandments are to be taken very seriously; when we strive to live them, we experience joy and peace that no one other than a loving God could create.

> The Ten Commandments, in their fundamental content, state grave obligations. However, obedience to these precepts also implies obligations in matter which is, in itself, light. (CCC 2081)

> **NOW THE RULER OF THIS WORLD WILL BE DRIVEN OUT, SAYS THE LORD; AND WHEN I AM LIFTED UP FROM THE EARTH, I WILL DRAW EVERYONE TO MYSELF.**
>
> JOHN 12:31B–32

How familiar am I with the Church's teaching regarding Mary's perpetual virginity? What are some ways I might deepen my appropriation of the faith in this regard?

Some Christians assert that Mary had biological children in addition to Jesus. How might I help dispel this misconception?

St. Bede, you lived in a time when the Gospel was spreading, although not without resistance. Please pray that I'll persevere in proclaiming Jesus and inviting others to live in a disciple relationship with Him for the glory of God and the salvation of souls. Amen.

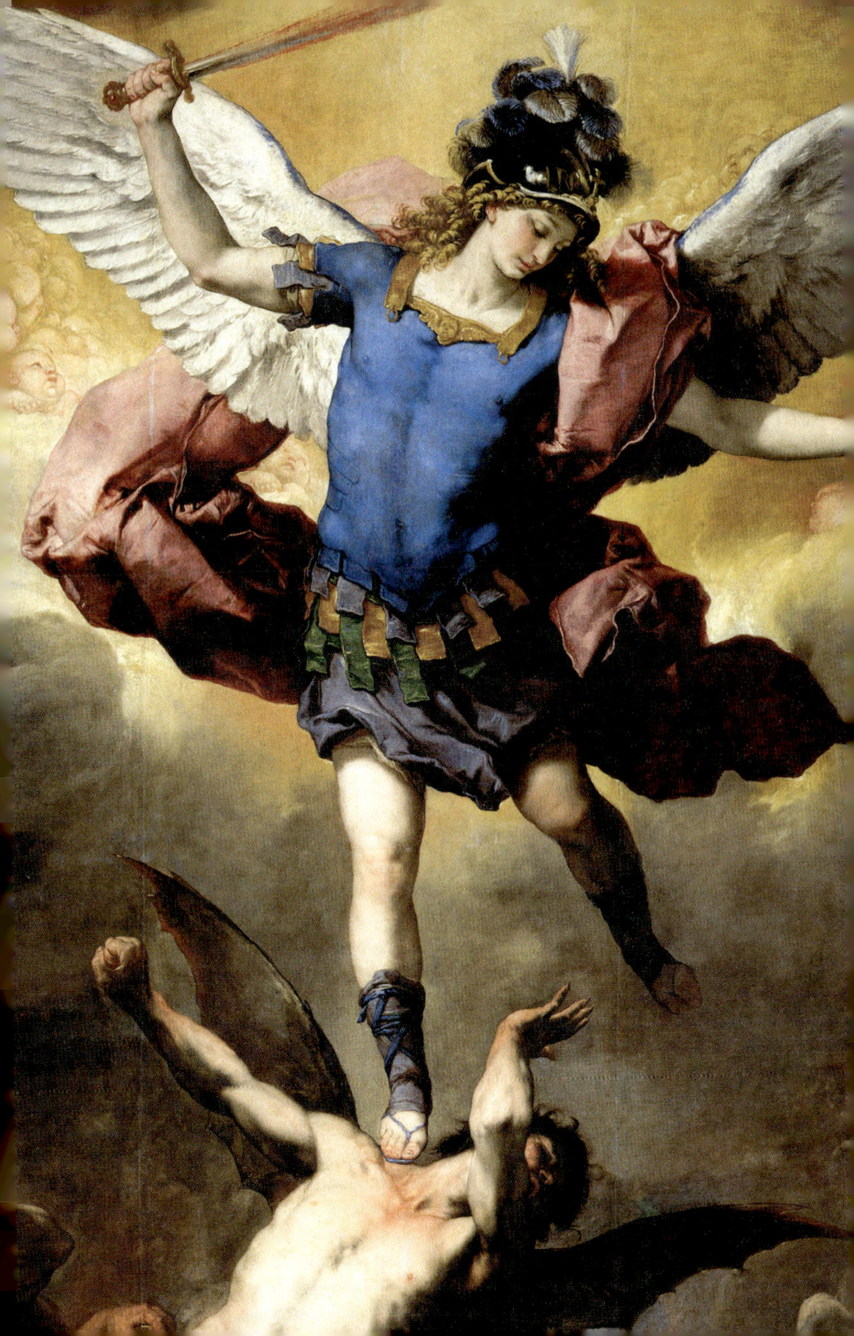

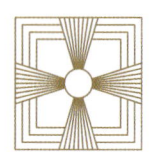

Eleventh Sunday in Ordinary Time

EZEKIEL 17:22–24

PSALM 92:2–3, 13–14, 15–16

2 CORINTHIANS 5:6–10

MARK 4:26–34

Fruits of Faith

Through the oracles of the prophet Ezekiel, God gave His people reason to hope. It would have been a cryptic message to Ezekiel's hearers receiving it long centuries before the Lord's coming. Ezekiel glimpsed a day when the Lord God would place a tree on a mountain in Israel, a tree that would "put forth branches and bear fruit." Who could have predicted that the tree would be a cross on the hill of Calvary and that the fruit would be salvation?

Ezekiel foresees salvation coming to "birds of every kind"—thus, not just to the chosen people of Israel but also to the Gentiles, who will "take wing" through their new life in Christ. God indeed will "lift high the lowly tree," as He solemnly promises at the conclusion of the passage from the prophet.

Such salvation surpasses humanity's most ambitious dreams. And so we express our gratitude in the Responsorial Psalm: "Lord, it is good to give thanks to you." It is indeed good to give thanks, and it is better still to give thanks with praise. The Psalmist speaks of those who are just upon the earth, but he looks to God as the source and measure of justice, of righteousness. Like Ezekiel, he evokes the image of a flourishing tree to describe the lives of the just. The image, again, suggests the Cross as the measure of righteousness.

The Cross is a challenge to those who would rather "flourish" according to worldly terms. It is a sign of contradiction. And so St. Paul repeatedly emphasizes to the Corinthians the necessity of courage. Our faith makes us strong, and it is proved in our deeds. The Apostle reminds us that we will be judged by the ways our faith manifests itself in works: "so that each may receive recompense, according to what he did in the body, whether good or evil."

Faith. Courage. God Himself will empower the works he expects from us; though we may freely choose to correspond to His grace. In the prophetic oracles, in the psalms that were sung in Jerusalem, He scattered the small seed that sprang up and became the mustard tree, large enough to accommodate all the birds of the sky, just as Ezekiel had foretold.

He gave this doctrine to His disciples, as He still does today, in terms they were able to understand, and He provided a full explanation. In the sacraments He provides still more: the grace of faith and the courage we need to live in the world as children of God.

When the grain is ripe, Jesus will use the sickle. Jesus will judge the living and dead based on faithful citizenship in God's kingdom. Sometimes what seems insignificant to several kings and rulers of this world may, like the mustard seed, make an enormous difference in terms of our eternity.

> When he comes at the end of time to judge the living and the dead, the glorious Christ will reveal the secret disposition of hearts

and will render to each man according to his works, and according to his acceptance or refusal of grace. (CCC 682)

In God's kingdom, human life and concern for its respect—for the dignity of each person without exception—receives a very high priority. And although this kingdom is never fully realized during our earthly life, we are obliged to take steps that will provide shelter, shade, and sustenance for as many people as feasible.

> The dignity of the human person requires the pursuit of the common good. Everyone should be concerned to create and support institutions that improve the conditions of human life. (CCC 1926)

THE SEED IS THE WORD OF GOD, CHRIST IS THE SOWER. ALL WHO COME TO HIM WILL LIVE FOREVER.

LUKE 8:11–12

Knowing that the secret disposition of my heart is known to Jesus, what in my heart is most in need of positive change?

What examples of the common good being pursued do I see in my communities? How might I help at least a bit more in this pursuit?

St. Paul, as you proclaimed Jesus to the Gentiles—expanding God's family like a rapidly growing, beautiful tree—pray that I'll allow our heavenly Father to work in and through me as He draws all people to the heart of Jesus by the Holy Spirit's power. Amen.

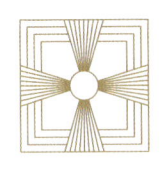

Twelfth Sunday in Ordinary Time

JOB 38:1, 8–11

PSALM 107:23–24, 25–26, 28–29, 30–31

2 CORINTHIANS 5:14–17

MARK 4:35–41

In the Storm

"Do you not yet have faith?" Our Lord's question in today's Gospel frames the Sunday liturgies for the remainder of the year, which the Church calls "Ordinary Time."

In the weeks ahead, the Church's liturgy will have us journeying with Jesus and His disciples, reliving their experience of His words and deeds, coming to know and believe in Him as they did.

Notice that today's Psalm almost provides an outline for the Gospel. We sing of sailors caught in a storm; in their desperation, they call to the Lord and He rescues them.

Mark's Gospel today also intends us to hear a strong echo of the story of the prophet Jonah. He, too, was found asleep on a boat when a life-threatening storm broke out that caused his fellow travelers to pray for deliverance, and then to marvel when the storm abated (see Jonah 1:3–16).

But Jesus is "something greater than Jonah" (Matthew 12:41). And Mark wants us to come to see what the Apostles saw—that God alone has the power to rebuke the wind and the sea (see Isaiah 50:2; Psalm 18:16). This is the point of today's First Reading.

If even the wind and sea obey Him, shouldn't we trust Him in the chaos and storms of our own lives? As with the Apostles, the Lord has asked each of us to cross to the other side, to leave behind our old ways to travel with Him in the little ship of the Church.

In their fear today, they call Him "Teacher." It is only faith in His teaching that can save us from perishing. And like

Christ—who was able to sleep through the storm, confident that His Father was with Him—we should trust in God (see Psalm 116:6; Romans 8:31).

As today's Epistle tells us, we are called to live in thanksgiving for our salvation as new creations, no longer for ourselves but for Him who died for our sake.

Jesus is Lord of creation. The fact that God created us in the first place shows Our Father's great love. Jesus, present from the beginning, fulfills God's ultimate plan and exercises loving dominion over all of creation. Even sea and wind obey our loving Lord Jesus.

> In the creation of the world and of man, God gave the first and universal witness to his almighty love and his wisdom, the first proclamation of the "plan of his loving goodness," which finds its goal in the new creation in Christ. (CCC 315)

Like Jesus' nature miracles, the miracle of the Most Holy Eucharist brings about some awe-inspiring effects. He whom the wind and sea obey can certainly pour out miraculous blessings through this great sacrament.

Communion with the Body and Blood of Christ increases the communicant's union with the Lord, forgives his venial sins, and preserves him from grave sins. Since receiving this sacrament strengthens the bonds of charity between the communicant and Christ, it also reinforces the unity of the Church as the Mystical Body of Christ. (CCC 1416)

How might I explain to another person the effects of receiving Holy Communion?

What indications in my community do I see of God's almighty love and wisdom? How might I help point these out to others more clearly?

Jesus, amidst the storms of my life, You provide the ultimate comfort food. Thank You for the Eucharist. Thank You for the spiritual nourishment, grace, and strength that Your Most Holy Body and Blood provide for me. I love You, Lord Jesus. Amen.

A GREAT PROPHET

HAS RISEN *in* OUR MIDST.

GOD HAS VISITED

HIS PEOPLE.

LUKE 7:16

Thirteenth Sunday in Ordinary Time

WISDOM 1:13–15; 2:23–24

PSALM 30:2, 4, 5–6, 11, 12, 13

2 CORINTHIANS 8:7, 9, 13–15

MARK 5:21–43 (OR 5:21–24, 35B–43)

Arise

God, who formed us in His imperishable image, did not intend for us to die, we hear in today's First Reading. Death entered the world through the devil's envy and Adam and Eve's sin; as a result, we are all bound to die. But in the moving story in today's Gospel, we see Jesus liberate a little girl from the possession of death.

On one level, Mark is recounting an event that led the disciples to understand Jesus' authority and power over even the final enemy, death (see 1 Corinthians 15:26). On another level, however, this episode is written to strengthen our hope that we also will be raised from the dead, along with all our loved ones who sleep in Christ (see 1 Corinthians 15:18).

Jesus commands the girl to "Arise!"—using the same Greek word the Apostles would later use to describe Jesus' own Resurrection (see Mark 16:6). And the consoling message of today's Gospel is that Jesus is the resurrection and the life. If we believe in Him, even though we die, we will live (see John 15:25–26).

We are called to have the same faith as the parents in the Gospel today—praying for our loved ones, trusting in Jesus' promise that even death cannot keep us apart. Notice the parents follow Him even though those in their own house tell them there is no hope and even though others ridicule Jesus' claim that the dead have only fallen asleep (see 1 Thessalonians 4:13–18).

Already in Baptism we've been raised to new life in Christ. And the Eucharist, like the food given to the little girl today, is the pledge that He will raise us on the last day.

We should rejoice, as we sing in today's Psalm, that He has brought us up from the netherworld, the pit of death. And, as Paul exhorts in today's Epistle, we should offer our lives in thanksgiving for this gracious act, imitating Christ in our love and generosity for others.

If this child were not dead, it would be appropriate in our time for a priest to administer the Sacrament of Anointing of the Sick. This sacrament is certainly not to be reserved only for times when death is imminent. Acting in the Person of Christ, priests anoint the seriously ill so that, if God wills it, they may get well and live.

> Each time a Christian falls seriously ill, he may receive the Anointing of the Sick, and also when, after he has received it, the illness worsens. (CCC 1529)

God's Son commands a little girl to arise. His healing grace allows this to occur. God does not command the impossible. Grace helps us fulfill His commandments.

What God commands he makes possible by his grace. (CCC 2082)

OUR SAVIOR JESUS CHRIST DESTROYED DEATH AND BROUGHT LIFE TO LIGHT THROUGH THE GOSPEL.

CF. 2 TIMOTHY 1:10

Have I ever been ridiculed for my faith? What was my reaction? How does Jesus react in this Gospel passage? How might I become more like Him in this respect?

Have I ever been guilty of ridiculing another for her or his faith? What are the consequences of this kind of behavior? How can I be more loving toward Christians and people of other faiths?

Heavenly Father, You heal me and give me new life throughout my earthly pilgrimage. Bless my family and friends, including those whose journey on earth has drawn to a close. Keep me in Your loving care until all the faithful are united in Your glorious presence forever. Amen.

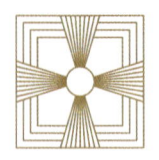

Fourteenth Sunday in Ordinary Time

EZEKIEL 2:2–5

PSALM 123:1–2, 2, 3–4

2 CORINTHIANS 12:7–10

MARK 6:1–6

Son of Mary

As we've walked with the Apostles in the Gospels in recent weeks, we've witnessed Jesus command the wind and sea. We've seen Him order a little girl to arise from the dead. But He seems to meet His match in His hometown of Nazareth. Today's Gospel is blunt: "He was not able to perform any mighty deed there."

Why not? Because of the people's lack of faith. They acknowledged the wisdom of His words, the power of His works. But they refused to recognize Him as a prophet come among them, a messenger sent by God. All they could see was how much "this man" was like them—a carpenter, the son of their neighbor, Mary, with brothers and sisters.

Of course, Mary was ever-virgin, and had no other children. The Gospel refers to Jesus' brothers as Paul refers to all Israelites as his brothers, the children of Abraham (see Romans 9:3, 7). That's the point in today's Gospel, too. Like the prophet Ezekiel in today's First Reading, Jesus was sent by God to the rebellious house of Israel, where He found His own brothers and sisters obstinate of heart and in revolt against God.

The servant is not above the Master (see Matthew 10:24). As His disciples, we, too, face the mockery and contempt we hear of in today's Psalm. And isn't it often hardest to live our faith among those in our own families, those who think they really know us, who define us by the people we used to be—before we chose to walk with Jesus?

As Paul confides in today's Epistle, insults and hardships are God's way of teaching us to rely solely on His grace. Jesus will work no mighty deeds in our lives unless we abandon ourselves to Him in faith.

Blessed, then, are those who take no offense in Him (see Luke 7:23). Instead, we must look upon Him with the eyes of servants, knowing that the son of Mary is also the Lord enthroned in the heavens.

There are several theories about references to sisters and brothers of Jesus, even though we know that Mary herself never bore a child other than Jesus. The main point here is that when something at face value seems to contradict a Church teaching, it's important to dig a little deeper and get all the facts so that the truth of Church teaching is understood, communicated, and, in fact, spread.

> Mary "remained a virgin in conceiving her Son, a virgin in giving birth to him, a virgin in carrying him, a virgin in nursing him at her breast, always a virgin" (St. Augustine, *Serm.* 186, 1: PL 38, 999): with her whole being she is "the handmaid of the Lord" (*Lk* 1:38). (CCC 510)

Jesus regularly observed the Sabbath. As His friends and followers, we celebrate His Resurrection on the Lord's Day, Sunday. In order to imitate Him and deepen our relationship with Him, we observe the Lord's Day and all that it entails.

> The Church celebrates the day of Christ's Resurrection on the "eighth day," Sunday, which is rightly called the Lord's Day (cf. SC 106). (CCC 2191)

THE SPIRIT OF THE LORD IS UPON ME, FOR HE SENT ME TO BRING GLAD TIDINGS TO THE POOR.

CF. LUKE 4:18

Have I ever heard someone make derogatory remarks about Mary? What are some ways I might help others better understand Mary's importance and great love for us all?

Along with helping out in the broader community, how am I at offering my time, talent, and treasure in my parish and at my home?

> *Most Blessed Virgin Mary, as you and St. Joseph took the boy Jesus to worship faithfully each week, pray that each disciple of your Son makes worshipping Him on the Lord's Day a priority. I pray that the liturgy deepens my relationship of love with Jesus, lighting my lifelong walk with your Son. Amen.*

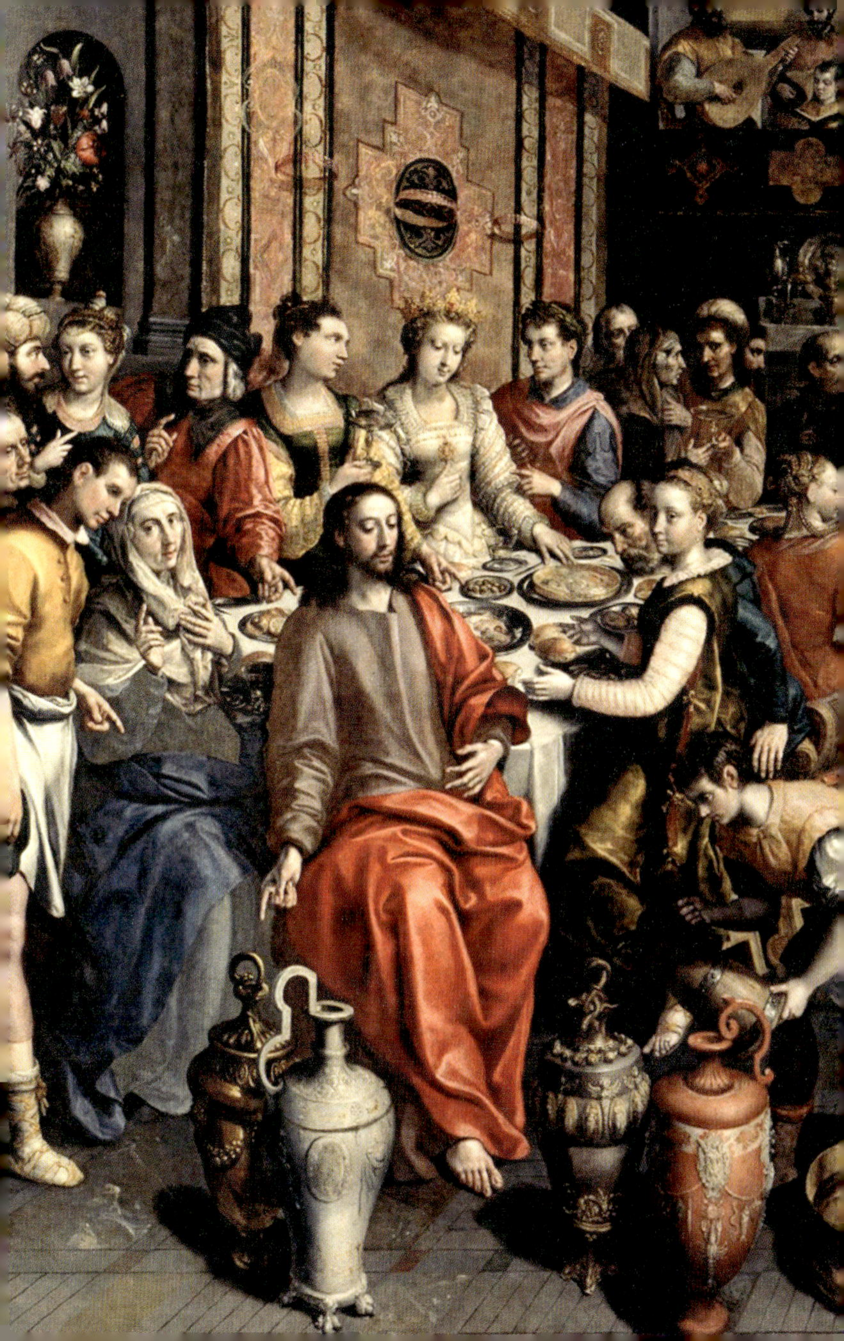

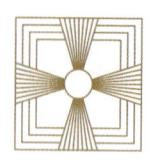

Fifteenth Sunday in Ordinary Time

AMOS 7:12–15

PSALM 85:9–10, 11–12, 13–14

EPHESIANS 1:3–14 (OR 1:3–10)

MARK 6:7–13

The Church's Mission

In commissioning the Apostles in today's Gospel, Jesus gives them—and us—a preview of His Church's mission after the Resurrection. His instructions to the Twelve echo those of God to the twelve tribes of Israel on the eve of their exodus from Egypt. The Israelites likewise were sent out with no bread and only one set of clothes, wearing sandals and carrying a staff (see Exodus 12:11; Deuteronomy 8:2–4). Like the Israelites, the Apostles are to rely solely on the providence of God and His grace.

Perhaps, also, Mark wants us to see the Apostles' mission, the mission of the Church, as that of leading a new exodus—delivering people from their exile from God and bringing them to the promised land, the kingdom of heaven.

Like Amos in today's First Reading, the Apostles are not "professionals," who earn their bread by prophesying. Like Amos, they are simply men (see Acts 14:15) summoned from their ordinary jobs and sent by God to be shepherds of their brothers and sisters.

Again this week we hear the theme of rejection: Amos experiences it, and Jesus warns the Apostles that some will not welcome or listen to them. The Church is called not necessarily to be successful but only to be faithful to God's command.

With the authority and power given to her by Jesus, the Church proclaims God's peace and salvation to those who believe in Him, as we sing in today's Psalm.

This word of truth, this gospel of salvation, is addressed to each of us personally, as Paul proclaims in today's Epistle. In the mystery of God's will, we have been chosen from before the foundation of the world to be His sons and daughters, to live for the praise of His glory.

Let us, then, give thanks for the Church today and for the spiritual blessings God has bestowed upon us. Let us resolve to further the Church's mission—to help others hear the call to repentance and welcome Christ into their lives.

Jesus sent the Twelve. He gave them special authority and instructions. Although democracy has proven itself to be an effective means of civil government, and although there are certainly some elements of the democratic process in our Catholic Church (e.g., papal election by cardinals), we should recall that from the Church's infancy special authority was given the Apostles by Jesus Himself. The Spirit-guided men who fill this unique leadership role today are our bishops.

> The Bishops, established by the Holy Spirit, succeed the apostles. They are "the visible source and foundation of unity in their own particular Churches" (*LG* 23). (CCC 938)

"They anointed with oil many who were sick" (Mark 6:13). This practice—this grace-filled anointing—continues today each time the Sacrament of Anointing of the Sick is celebrated. When a priest or bishop liturgically prays for the unique grace that this sacrament offers, his holy anointing facilitates an encounter with the soothing, often healing, Person of Jesus.

> The celebration of the Anointing of the Sick consists essentially in the anointing of the forehead and hands of the sick person (in the Roman Rite) or of other parts of the body (in the Eastern rite), the anointing being accompanied by the liturgical prayer of the celebrant asking for the special grace of this sacrament. (CCC 1531)

MAY THE FATHER OF OUR LORD JESUS CHRIST ENLIGHTEN THE EYES OF OUR HEARTS, THAT WE MAY KNOW WHAT IS THE HOPE THAT BELONGS TO OUR CALL.

CF. EPHESIANS 1:17–18

What comes to mind when I ponder the fact that my bishop is a successor to the original Apostles?

What are some of my bishop's priorities? (Often these are described on diocesan websites.) How might I help my bishop pursue those goals he currently considers most important in the diocese?

St. John Paul II, please pray that the Church will continue being an integral part of my disciple relationship with Jesus. Please pray also that all disciples answer God's call to full communion with the Mystical Body of Christ, His holy Church.

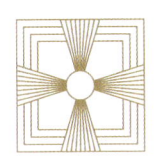

Sixteenth Sunday in Ordinary Time

JEREMIAH 23:1–16

PSALM 23:1–3, 3–4, 5, 6

EPHESIANS 2:13–18

MARK 6:30–34

One Flock

As the Twelve return from their first missionary journey in today's Gospel, our readings continue to reflect on the authority and mission of the Church.

Jeremiah says in the First Reading that Israel's leaders, through godlessness and fanciful teachings, have misled and scattered God's people. He promises God will send a shepherd, a king and son of David, to gather the lost sheep and appoint for them new shepherds (see Ezekiel 34:23).

The crowd gathering on the green grass (see Mark 6:39) in today's Gospel is the start of the remnant that Jeremiah promised would be brought back to the meadow of Israel. The people seem to sense that Jesus is the Lord, the Good Shepherd (see John 10:11), the king they've been waiting for (see Hosea 3:1–5). Jesus is moved to pity, seeing them as sheep without a shepherd. This phrase was used by Moses to describe Israel's need for a shepherd to succeed him (see Numbers 27:17). And as Moses appointed Joshua, Jesus appointed the Twelve to continue shepherding His people on earth.

Jesus had said there were other sheep who did not belong to Israel's fold, but who would hear His voice and be joined to the one flock of the one Shepherd (see John 10:16). In God's plan, the Church is to seek out first the lost sheep of the house of Israel and then to bring all nations into the fold (see Acts 13:26; Romans 1:16). Paul, too, in today's Epistle, sees the Church as a new creation in which those nations who were once far off from God are joined as "one new person" with the children of Israel.

As we sing in today's Psalm, through the Church, the Lord, our Good Shepherd, still leads people to the verdant pastures of the kingdom, to the restful waters of Baptism; He still anoints with the oil of Confirmation and spreads the Eucharistic table before all people, filling their cups to overflowing.

The Apostles needed a day of recollection. Their hearts, minds, bodies and souls needed to rest a while. Time for prayer helps us to learn from the Master Teacher. Whether it's speaking to God (vocal prayer), reflecting on something He said (meditation), or simply and wordlessly enjoying His presence (contemplation), making time to pray keeps us focused on what and Who truly gives us life.

> The Christian tradition comprises three major expressions of the life of prayer: vocal prayer, meditation, and contemplative prayer. They have in common the recollection of the heart. (CCC 2721)

The Sacred Heart of Jesus felt pity for the crowd. They had a right to know the truth about life—both earthly and eternal.

They had a dignity that wasn't being lived out fully. Jesus respects us too much to let us live in darkness; so, through His Church, He teaches us many things.

> Respect for the human person considers the other "another self." It presupposes respect for the fundamental rights that flow from the dignity intrinsic of the person. (CCC 1944)

How might I move toward practicing contemplative prayer? (Bear in mind that this differs dramatically from the "mind-emptying" approach to meditation you may have encountered.)

Who do I know that is like sheep without a shepherd? While recalling that I myself am in need of shepherding, how might I help this person or these people get the guidance they need?

Jesus, You are the Good Shepherd. Thank You for laying down Your life for me. Please help me always to live up to my dignity as a beloved child of God and to honor the God-given dignity of each person. Amen.

MY SHEEP HEAR MY VOICE,

SAYS *the* LORD;

I KNOW THEM,

AND THEY FOLLOW ME.

JOHN 10:27

Seventeenth Sunday in Ordinary Time

2 KINGS 4:42–44

PSALM 145:10–11, 15–16, 17–18

EPHESIANS 4:1–6

JOHN 6:1–15

Bread Left Over

Today's liturgy brings together several strands of Old Testament expectation to reveal Jesus as Israel's promised Messiah and king, the Lord who comes to feed His people.

Notice the parallels between today's Gospel and First Reading. Both Elisha and Jesus face a crowd of hungry people with only a few barley loaves. We hear similar words about how impossible it will be to feed the crowd with so little. And in both, the miraculous multiplication of bread satisfies the hungry and leaves food left over.

The Elisha story looks back to Moses, the prophet who fed God's people in the wilderness (see Exodus 16). Moses prophesied that God would send a prophet like him (see Deuteronomy 18:15–19). The crowd in today's Gospel, witnessing His miracle, identifies Jesus as that prophet.

The Gospel today again shows Jesus to be the Lord, the Good Shepherd, who makes His people lie down on green grass and spreads a table before them (see Psalm 23:2, 5). The miraculous feeding is a sign that God has begun to fulfill the promise we sing of in today's Psalm: to give His people food in due season and satisfy their desire (see Psalm 81:16).

But Jesus points to the final fulfillment of that promise in the Eucharist. He does the same things He does at the Last Supper—He takes the loaves, pronounces a blessing of thanksgiving (literally, "eucharist"), and gives the bread to the people (see Matthew 26:26). Notice, too, that twelve baskets of bread are left over, one for each of the Apostles.

These are signs that should point us to the Eucharist, in which the Church founded on the Apostles continues to feed us with the living bread of His Body. In this Eucharist, we are made one body with the Lord, as we hear in today's Epistle. Let us resolve again, then, to live lives worthy of such a great calling.

Jesus could have distributed this food in a variety of ways. Yet He Himself took, blessed, broke, and gave the loaves to the people. Today, through our priests, Jesus offers His sacrifice of thanks and praise, giving us Himself as the Bread of Life.

> It is Christ himself, the eternal high priest of the New Covenant who, acting through the ministry of the priests, offers the Eucharistic sacrifice. And it is the same Christ, really present under the species of bread and wine, who is the offering of the Eucharistic sacrifice. (CCC 1410)

The Lord wanted nothing to be wasted. Squandering resources is irresponsible, disrespectful, and bothersome to God. We have a moral obligation to use creation's bounty wisely, both for present purposes and with respect to future generations.

The dominion granted by the Creator over the mineral, vegetable, and animal resources of the universe cannot be separated from respect for moral obligations, including those toward generations to come. (CCC 2456)

A GREAT PROPHET HAS RISEN IN OUR MIDST. GOD HAS VISITED HIS PEOPLE.
LUKE 7:16

What does the fact that Christ Himself offers the Eucharistic sacrifice have to do with who receives the sacrament of Holy Orders?

How might one abuse dominion over resources? What are some suitable ways I can show respect for future generations regarding our universe's resources?

God of all creation, loving Creator of every person, place, and thing, help me to realize my need for Your grace. Help me to use all of Your gifts wisely, for my benefit and that of future generations. Amen.

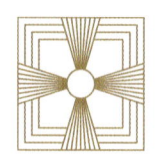

Eighteenth Sunday in Ordinary Time

EXODUS 16:2–4, 12–15

PSALM 78:3–4, 23–24, 25, 54

EPHESIANS 4:17, 20–24

JOHN 6:24–35

Endurance Test

The journey of discipleship is a lifelong exodus from the slavery of sin and death to the holiness of truth in Mount Zion, the promised land of eternal life.

The road can get rough. And when it does, we can be tempted to complain like the Israelites in this week's First Reading. We have to see these times of hardship as a test of what is in our hearts, a call to trust God more and purify the motives for our faith (see Deuteronomy 8:2–3). As Paul reminds us in this week's Epistle, we must leave behind our old self-deceptions and desires and live according to the likeness of God in which we are made.

Jesus tells the crowd in this week's Gospel that they are following Him for the wrong reasons. They seek Him because He filled their bellies. The Israelites also were content to follow God so long as there was plenty of food. Food is the most obvious of signs—because it is the most basic of our human needs. We need our daily bread to live. But we cannot live by this bread alone. We need the bread of eternal life that preserves those who believe in Him (see Wisdom 16:20, 26).

The manna in the wilderness, like the bread Jesus multiplied for the crowd, was a sign of God's Providence—that we should trust that He will provide. These signs pointed to their fulfillment in the Eucharist, the abundant bread of angels we sing about in this week's Psalm.

This is the food that God longs to give us. This is the bread we should be seeking. But too often we don't ask for this bread. Instead, we seek the perishable stuff of our everyday wants and anxieties. In our weakness, we think these things are what we really need. We have to trust God more. If we seek first His kingdom and His righteousness, all these things will be ours as well (see Matthew 6:33).

Jesus isn't shy in this Gospel passage. He clearly communicates His importance and, in the process, alludes to the Eucharist. The importance of the Eucharist is crystal clear in our Catholic faith. A bishop, above all other duties related to worship, must see to it that the Eucharist is available and celebrated throughout his diocese in accordance with the resources accessible to him.

> Helped by the priests, their co-workers, and by the deacons, the bishops have the duty of authentically teaching the faith, celebrating divine worship, above all the Eucharist, and guiding their Churches as true pastors. Their responsibility also includes concern for all the Churches, with and under the Pope.
> (CCC 939)

Sometimes we eat and are filled. Other times, we receive our fair share on any given day and may be less than full. But we are always entitled to be treated fairly so that we have a reasonable chance to obtain sufficient resources for ourselves and any dependents. This is justice in the societal setting.

> Society ensures social justice by providing the conditions that allow associations and individuals to obtain their due. (CCC 1943)

ONE DOES NOT LIVE BY BREAD ALONE, BUT BY EVERY WORD THAT COMES FORTH FROM THE MOUTH OF GOD.

MATTHEW 4:4B

How is Jesus the Bread of Life?

In what ways do I contribute to providing conditions that allow individuals and associations to get their due?

Jesus, You are Priest, Prophet, and King. Deepen my trust in You, I pray, that I may always seek first the kingdom of God and His righteousness. Amen.

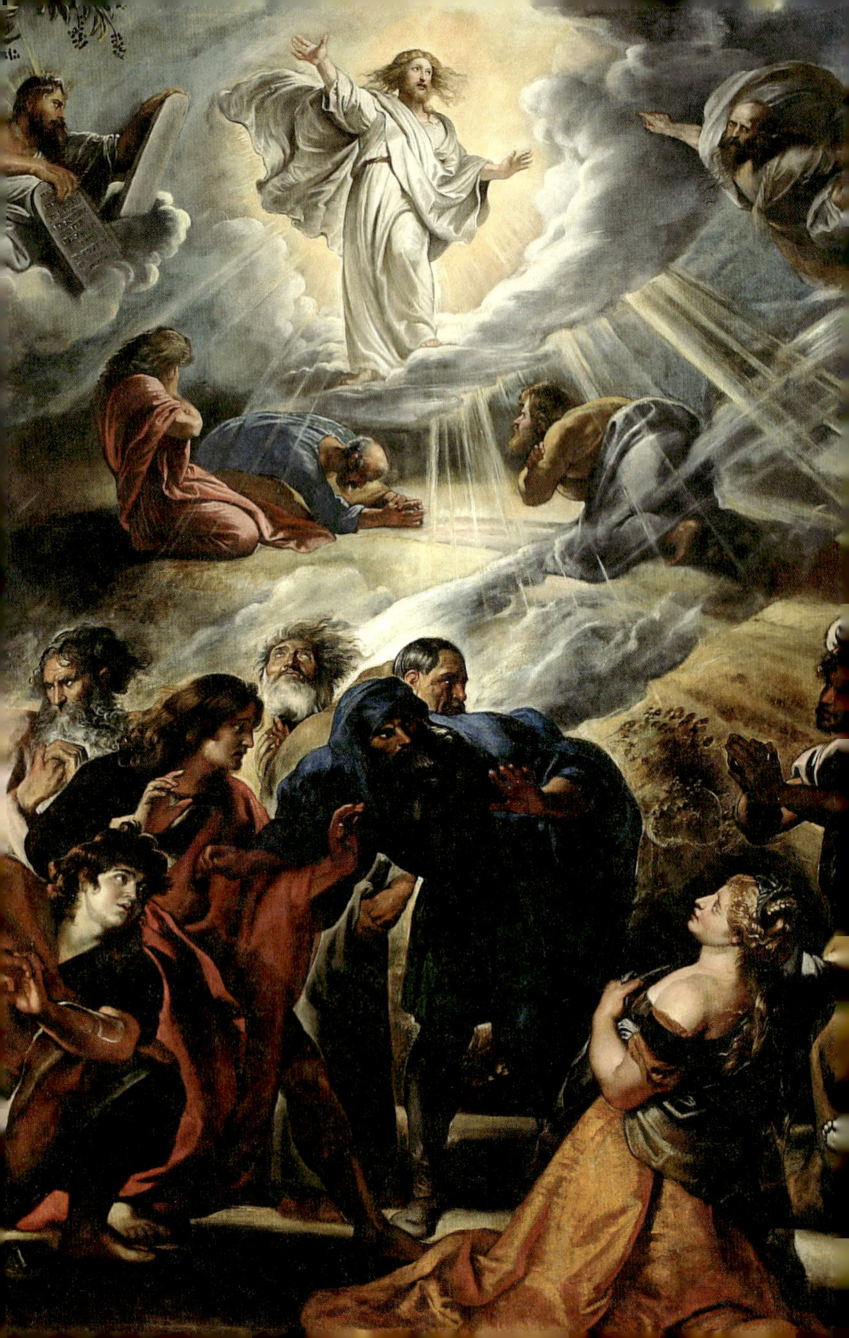

Transfiguration of the Lord

DANIEL 7:9–10, 13–14

PSALM 97:1–2, 5–6, 9

2 PETER 1:16–19

MARK 9:2–10

Majestic Voice

High on the holy mountain in today's Gospel, the true identity of Jesus is fully revealed in His Transfiguration. Standing between Moses and the prophet Elijah, Jesus is the bridge that joins the Law of Moses to the prophets and psalms (see Luke 24:24–27). As Moses did, Jesus climbs a mountain with three friends who are named specifically in the Scripture and beholds God's glory in a cloud (see Exodus 24:1, 9, 15). As Elijah did, He hears God's voice on the mountain (see 1 Kings 19:8–19).

Elijah was prophesied to return as the herald of the Messiah and the Lord's new covenant (see Malachi 3:1, 23–24). Jesus is revealed today as that Messiah. By His death and Resurrection, which He intimates today to the Apostles, He makes a new covenant with all creation.

The majestic voice declares Jesus to be God's own beloved Son, in whom the Father is well pleased (see Psalm 2:7). God here gives us a glimpse of His inner life. In the cloud of the Holy Spirit, the Father reveals His love for the Son and invites us to share in that love as His beloved sons and daughters.

Shadowed by the clouds of heaven, His clothes dazzling white, Jesus is the Son of Man whom Daniel foresees being enthroned in today's First Reading.

He is the king, the Lord of all the earth, as we sing in today's Psalm. But is He truly the Lord of our hearts and minds?

The last word God speaks from heaven today is a command: "Listen to him" (see Deuteronomy 18:15–19). The word of the Lord should be like a lamp shining in the darkness of our days, as Peter tells us in today's First Reading.

How well are we listening? Do we attend to His Word each day? Let us today rededicate ourselves to listening. Let us hear Him as the word of life, the bright morning star of divine life waiting to arise in our hearts (see Revelation 2:28; 22:16).

What does rising from the dead mean? Why are folks obsessed with zombies and such? Maybe it's because we know, deep inside, that life goes on after our earthly pilgrimage ends. Resurrection isn't resuscitation. Jesus rose gloriously and victoriously from the dead.

> Faith in the Resurrection has as its object an event which is historically attested to by the disciples, who really encountered the Risen One. At the same time, this event is mysteriously transcendent insofar as it is the entry of Christ's humanity into the glory of God. (CCC 656)

"Listen to him." Jesus doesn't confuse love with permissiveness, as we often do. The Son of Man shared clear teaching about good and evil, about what we *should* do versus what we *can* do. The Transfiguration of the Lord makes clear that Jesus is who He says He is—the beloved Son of God. Let's listen to Him, especially as He speaks to us in a well-formed conscience.

> Man is obliged to follow the moral law, which urges him "to do what is good and avoid what is evil" (cf. *GS* 16). This law makes itself heard in his conscience. (CCC 1713)

How might I occasionally confuse happiness with pleasure, love with permissiveness, what I should do with what I can do? What can I ask of God that will help me benefit from clarity on these important distinctions?

Remembering that no one can argue with my testimony because it's simply an account of my experiences, how might I witness to others about my encounters with the Risen One?

SS. Peter, James, and John, as you were blessed with a preview of Jesus in His glory—as He would appear when He was raised from the dead—pray that the historical reality of Christ's Resurrection will be acknowledged by all people and that all will listen to Him as His disciples. Amen.

THIS IS MY BELOVED SON,

WITH WHOM I AM WELL

PLEASED; LISTEN *to* HIM.

MATTHEW 17:5C

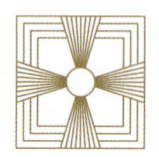

Nineteenth Sunday in Ordinary Time

1 KINGS 19:4–8

PSALM 34:2–3, 4–5, 6–7, 8–9

EPHESIANS 4:30–5:2

JOHN 6:41–51

Take and Eat

Sometimes we feel like Elijah in today's First Reading. We want to lie down and die, keenly aware of our failures—that we seem to be getting no better at doing what God wants of us. We can be tempted to despair, as the prophet was on his forty-day journey in the desert. We can be tempted to "murmur" against God, as the Israelites did during their forty years in the desert (see Exodus 16:2, 7, 8; 1 Corinthians 10:10).

The Gospel today uses the same word, "murmur," to describe the crowds, who reenact Israel's hardheartedness in the desert. Jesus tells them that prophecies are being fulfilled in Him, that they are being taught by God. But they can't believe it. They can only see His flesh, that He is the "son" of Joseph and Mary.

Yet, if we believe, if we seek Him in our distress, He will deliver us from our fears, as we sing in today's Psalm.

At the altar in every Eucharist, the angel of the Lord, the Lord Himself (see Exodus 3:1–2), touches us. He commands us to take and eat His flesh given for the life of the world (see Matthew 26:26). This taste of the heavenly gift (see Hebrews 6:4–5) comes to us with a renewed command to get up and continue on the journey we began with our baptism—the journey to the mountain of God, the kingdom of heaven. He will give us the Bread of Life, the strength and grace we need, just as He fed our spiritual ancestors in the wilderness and Elijah in the desert.

So let us stop grieving the Spirit of God, as Paul says in today's Epistle, in another reference to Israel in the desert (see Isaiah 63:10). Let us like Elijah say to God, "Take my life." Let us say it, though, not in the sense of wanting to die but in giving ourselves as a sacrificial offering, loving Him as He has loved us on the Cross and in the Eucharist.

None of us has seen the Father. God is, in a sense, invisible. Yet, those who met Jesus got a glimpse of divinity. And as we become more Christlike, we show the world that God is real, even though a leap of faith is required to allow ourselves to be drawn to the Father, to be taught by Him, to receive God into our heart and home.

> Man is predestined to reproduce the image of God's Son made man, the "image of the invisible God" (*Col* 1:15), so that Christ shall be the first-born of a multitude of brothers and sisters (cf. *Eph* 1:3–6; *Rom* 8:29). (CCC 381)

To justify our life entirely to God would be an impossibility. We all fall short and need to be renewed by God's grace. Placing our faith in the Father, believing the effectiveness of Jesus' sacrifice, adhering to the ordinary means of salvation revealed by our Triune God—these acquire for us justification and, ultimately, eternal life.

Justification includes the remission of sins, sanctification, and the renewal of the inner man. (CCC 2019)

I AM THE LIVING BREAD
THAT CAME DOWN FROM HEAVEN,
SAYS THE LORD; WHOEVER EATS THIS
BREAD WILL LIVE FOREVER.

JOHN 6:51

In what ways does God teach me?

How much "murmuring" do I do? In what ways might I use my gift of speech more constructively?

St. Joseph, as your righteous life was made possible by God's grace and mercy, pray for my perseverance, strength, holiness, and ongoing renewal as a faithful disciple of your foster Son, my Savior, Jesus. Amen.

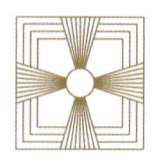

Twentieth Sunday in Ordinary Time

PROVERBS 9:1–6

PSALM 34:2–3, 4–5, 6–7

EPHESIANS 5:15–20

JOHN 6:51–58

Wisdom's Feast

The Wisdom of God has prepared a feast, we hear in today's First Reading. We must become like children (see Matthew 18:3–4) to hear and accept this invitation. For it is in every Eucharist that the folly of the Cross is represented and renewed.

To the world, it is foolishness to believe that the crucified Jesus rose from the dead. And for many, as for the crowds in today's Gospel, it is foolishness—maybe even madness—to believe that Jesus can give us His flesh to eat.

Yet, Jesus repeats Himself with gathering intensity in the Gospel today. Notice the reiteration of the words "eat" and "drink," and "my flesh" and "my blood." To heighten the unbelievable realism of what Jesus asks us to believe, John in these verses uses not the ordinary Greek word for eating but a cruder term, once reserved to describe the "munching" of feeding animals.

The foolishness of God is wiser than human wisdom (see 1 Corinthians 1:18–25). In His foolish love, He chooses to save those who believe that His flesh is true food and His blood true drink.

Fear of the Lord, the desire to live by His will, is the beginning of true wisdom, Paul says in today's Epistle (see Proverbs 9:10). And as we sing in today's Psalm, those who fear Him shall not want for any good thing.

We are called again today in the liturgy to renew our faith in the Eucharist, to forsake the foolishness of believing only what we can see with our eyes.

We approach, then, not only an altar prepared with bread and wine but the feast of wisdom—the banquet of heaven—in which God our Savior renews His everlasting covenant and promises to destroy death forever (see Isaiah 25:6–9).

Let us make the most of our days, as Paul says, always, in the Eucharist, giving thanks to God for everything in the name of Jesus, the bread come down from heaven.

The Apostles were there when Jesus delivered the unambiguous words we hear today in the Gospel. They eventually came to know that one major uniting factor among the followers of Jesus is that of Holy Communion. Even today, amidst legitimate diversity, the witness of our Apostles and their successors, the bishops, helps draw all together in Jesus.

> The criterion that assures unity amid the diversity of liturgical traditions is fidelity to apostolic Tradition, i.e., the communion in the faith and the sacraments received from the apostles, a communion that is both signified and guaranteed by apostolic succession. (CCC 1209)

Not just anyone can effect the change that occurs in ordinary bread and wine, making them the Body, Blood, Soul, and

Divinity of Jesus. Those who were with Him from the beginning—the Apostles—were first to confect the Eucharist. Eventually, hands were laid on presbyters (priests) to help make this great sacrament more widely available.

> Only validly ordained priests can preside at the Eucharist and consecrate the bread and the wine so that they become the Body and Blood of the Lord. (CCC 1411)

What are the benefits of apostolic succession?

How might I explain my belief in the Real Presence of Jesus in the Eucharist to one who has yet to make that leap of faith?

St. Matthew, as Jesus drew you from being a despised tax collector to becoming a priest of the New Testament, pray that the nourishment I receive in the Eucharist will help transform me into an ever more Christlike disciple of our Master and Teacher, Jesus. Amen.

WHOEVER EATS MY FLESH

AND DRINKS MY BLOOD

REMAINS IN ME

AND I IN HIM,

SAYS *the* LORD.

JOHN 6:56

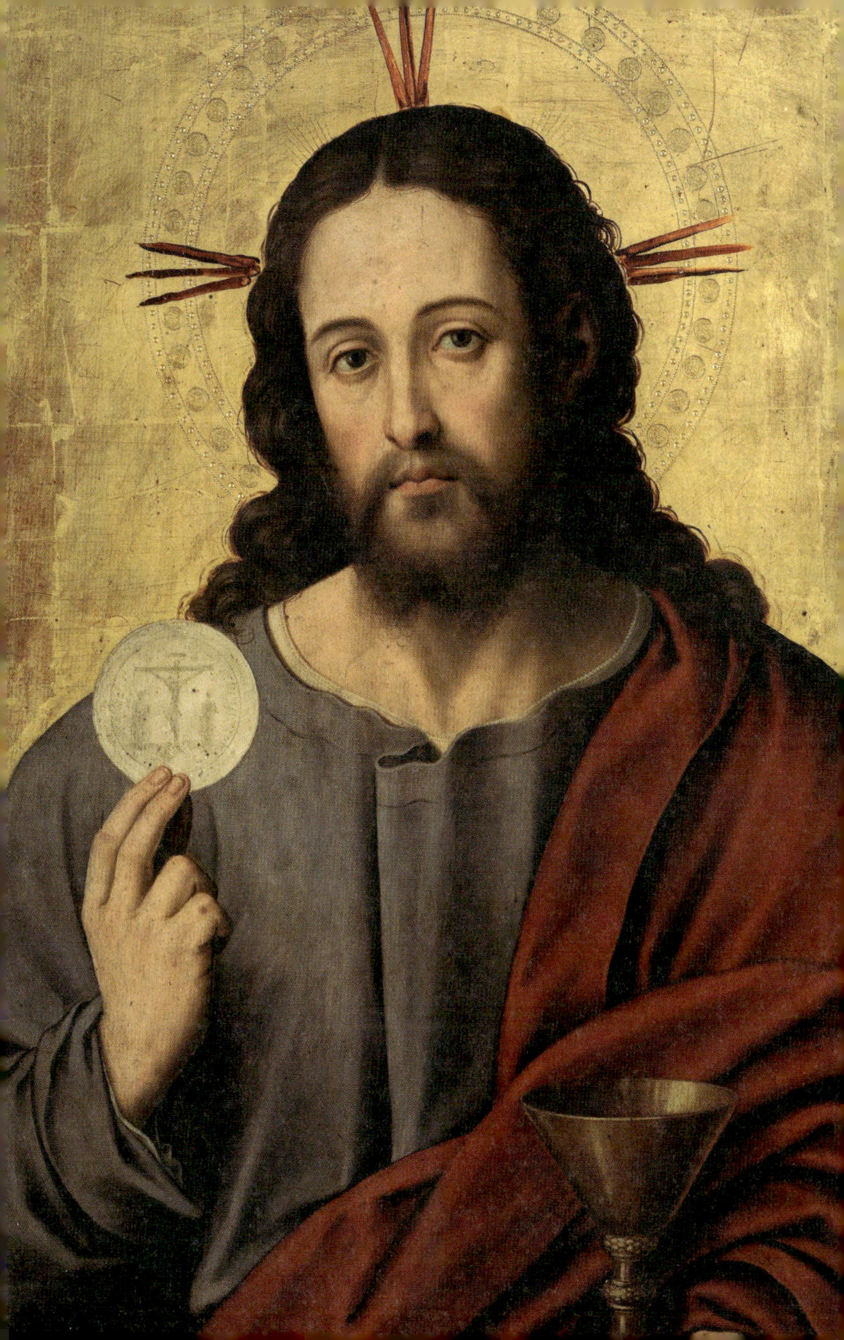

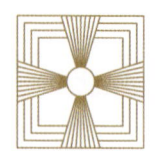

Twenty-First Sunday in Ordinary Time

JOSHUA 24:1–2A, 15–17, 18B

PSALM 34:2–3, 16–17, 18–19, 20–21

EPHESIANS 5:21–32 (OR 5:2A, 25–32)

JOHN 6:60–69

A Choice to Make

This Sunday's Mass readings conclude a four-week meditation on the Eucharist. The Twelve Apostles in today's Gospel are asked to make a choice—either to believe and accept the new covenant Jesus offers in His Body and Blood or return to their former ways of life.

Their choice is prefigured by the decision Joshua asks the twelve tribes to make in today's First Reading. Joshua gathers them at Shechem, where God first appeared to their father Abraham, promising to make his descendants a great nation in a new land (see Genesis 12:1–9). And he issues a blunt challenge: either renew their covenant with God or serve the alien gods of the surrounding nations.

We, too, are being asked today to decide whom we will serve. For four weeks, we have been presented in the liturgy with the mystery of the Eucharist—a daily miracle far greater than those performed by God in bringing the Israelites out of the land of Egypt.

He has promised us a new homeland, eternal life, and has offered us bread from heaven to strengthen us on our journey. He has told us that unless we eat His flesh and drink His blood we will have no life in us. It is a hard saying, as many murmur in today's Gospel. Yet, He has given us the words of eternal life.

We must believe, as Peter says today, that He is the Holy One of God, who handed Himself over for us, who gave His flesh for the life of the world. As we hear in today's Epistle, Jesus did this that we might be sanctified through the water and word of Baptism, by which we enter into His new covenant.

Through the Eucharist, He nourishes and cherishes us, making us His own flesh and blood, just as husband and wife become one flesh. Let us renew our covenant today, approaching the altar with confidence that, as we sing in today's Psalm, the Lord will redeem the lives of His servants.

What if we saw the Son of Man ascending to where He was before? We would have witnessed the Ascension of Jesus just as His disciples did. Jesus, the Holy One of God, is somehow with the Father physically with a glorified body. Bodily, Christ will come again.

> Christ's Ascension marks the definitive entrance of Jesus' humanity into God's heavenly domain, whence he will come again (cf. *Acts* 1:11); this humanity in the meantime hides him from the eyes of men (cf. *Col* 3:3). (CCC 665)

Faith isn't always easy to acquire or receive. Thankfully, we're not alone on our journey of faith. As the Twelve had each other in coming to believe Jesus' divinity, so we have our Church to accompany us as we strive to deepen and strengthen our belief.

"Believing" is an ecclesial act. The Church's faith precedes, engenders, supports and nourishes our faith. The Church is the mother of all believers. "No one can have God as Father who does not have the Church as Mother" (St. Cyprian, *De unit*. 6: PL 4, 519). (CCC 181)

YOUR WORDS, LORD, ARE SPIRIT AND LIFE; YOU HAVE THE WORDS OF EVERLASTING LIFE.

JOHN 6:63C, 68C

Where is Jesus right now?

Who in my community finds the teaching of Jesus to be a hard saying? How might I support them so that, in faith, they can accept it?

St. Peter, as you exclaimed that Jesus has the words of everlasting life, pray that I remain faithful to Him—encouraged within His Body, the Church—until He comes again in glory. Amen.

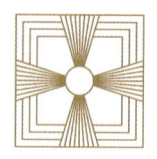

Twenty-Second Sunday in Ordinary Time

DEUTERONOMY 4:1–2, 6–8
PSALM 15:2–3, 3–4, 4–5
JAMES 1:17–18, 21B–22, 27
MARK 7:1–8, 14–15, 21–23

Pure Religion

Today's Gospel casts Jesus in a prophetic light, as one having authority to interpret God's law. Jesus' quotation from Isaiah today is ironic (see Isaiah 29:13). In observing the law, the Pharisees honor God by ensuring that nothing unclean passes their lips. In this, however, they've turned the law inside out, making it a matter of simply performing certain external actions.

The gift of the law, which we hear God giving to Israel in today's First Reading, is fulfilled in Jesus' Gospel, which shows us the law's true meaning and purpose (see Matthew 5:17): to form our hearts, to make us pure and therefore able to live in the Lord's presence. The law was given that we might live and enter into the inheritance promised to us—the kingdom of God, eternal life.

Israel, by its observance of the law, was meant to be an example to surrounding nations. As James tells us in today's Epistle, the Gospel was given to us that we might have new birth "by the word of truth." By living the Word we've received, we're to be examples of God's wisdom to those around us, the "firstfruits" of a new humanity.

This means we must be "doers" of the Word, not merely hearers of it. As we sing in today's Psalm and hear again in today's Epistle, we must work for justice, taking care of our brothers and sisters and living by the truth God has placed in our hearts.

The Word given to us is a perfect gift. We should not add to it through vain and needless devotions. Nor should we subtract from it by picking and choosing which of His laws to honor. "Hear me," Jesus says in today's Gospel. Today, we're called to examine our relationship to God's law. Is the practice of our religion a pure listening to Jesus, a humble welcoming of the Word planted in us and able to save our souls? Or are we only paying lip service?

The word "unchastity" appears in this Gospel passage. Jesus modeled all virtue, including that of chastity. In answering our call to live chastely, surrendering our hearts to the Lord of life and love will help keep them filled with peace from deep within.

> Christ is the model of chastity. Every baptized person is called to lead a chaste life, each according to his particular state of life. (CCC 2394)

What Jesus is describing, largely, is something called concupiscence. The Ninth Commandment reminds us that along with avoiding sinful behavior—perhaps as a helpful way of avoiding it—we should be mindful of our thoughts and feelings, always confidently asking God to cleanse our hearts with His grace.

The ninth commandment warns against lust or carnal concupiscence. (CCC 2529)

THE FATHER WILLED TO GIVE US BIRTH BY THE WORD OF TRUTH THAT WE MAY BE A KIND OF FIRSTFRUITS OF HIS CREATURES.

JAMES 1:18

What are the similarities and differences between Tradition with a capital T and "small t" tradition?

How does anything mentioned in Jesus' list of actions that defile a person affect those around me? What can I do to help minimize these effects?

Jesus, as You model chastity for us, please help me grow in self-control, modesty, purity, chastity, and all virtue—always by Your grace and mercy. Amen.

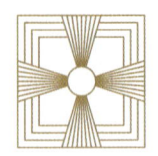

Twenty-Third Sunday in Ordinary Time

ISAIAH 35:4–7A

PSALM 146:6–7, 8–9, 9–10

JAMES 2:1–5

MARK 7:31–37

All Things Well

The incident in today's Gospel is recorded only by Mark. The key line is what the crowd says at the end: "He has done all things well." In the Greek, this echoes the creation story, recalling that God saw all the things he had done and declared them good (see Genesis 1:31).

Mark also deliberately evokes Isaiah's promise, which we hear in today's First Reading, that God will make the deaf hear and the mute speak. Mark even uses a Greek word to describe the man's condition (*mogilalon*, "speech impediment") that's only found in one other place in the Bible—in the Greek translation of today's Isaiah passage, where the prophet describes the "mute" singing.

The crowd recognizes that Jesus is doing what the prophet had foretold. But Mark wants us to see something far greater. He writes to show us that, to use the words from today's First Reading, "Here is your God."

Notice how personal and physical the drama is in the Gospel. Our focus is drawn to a hand, a finger, ears, a tongue, spitting. In Jesus, Mark shows us, God has truly come in the flesh.

What He has done is to make all things new, a new creation (see Revelation 21:1–5). As Isaiah promised, He has made the living waters of Baptism flow in the desert of the world. He has set captives free from their sins, as we sing in today's Psalm. He has come that rich and poor might dine together in the Eucharistic feast, as James tells us in today's Epistle.

He has done for each of us what He did for that replace with "man who was deaf and mute." He has opened our ears to hear the Word of God and loosed our tongues that we might sing praises to Him. Let us then, in the Eucharist, again give thanks to our glorious Lord Jesus Christ. Let us say with Isaiah, here is our God, He comes to save us. Let us be rich in faith, that we might inherit the kingdom promised to those who love Him.

Ordinary objects can sometimes point us toward God in a concrete way. Holy water in the font, touched lightly on to our forehead, heart, and shoulders. The crucifix on our blessed rosary reminding us of Jesus' love. A blessed palm displayed in our home—calling to mind how quickly fame can turn to persecution in a world where human hearts can shift positions all too easily.

These objects are called "sacramentals." Jesus knows that engaging our senses helps us encounter Him at deeper levels; He made use of this man's senses in curing him. Sacramentals can fill everyday life with sensory reminders of God's grace—readying us to receive this grace abundantly in one or more of the seven sacraments.

> Sacramentals are sacred signs instituted by the Church. They prepare men to receive the fruit of the sacraments and sanctify different circumstances of life. (CCC 1677)

As Jesus embodies His Father's goodness by doing all things well, so the Church He founded concretizes God's presence in our world and makes communion with Him accessible to all people. Astonishingly, salvation can actually be ours.

> The Church in this world is the sacrament of salvation, the sign and the instrument of the communion of God and men. (CCC 780)

Why did Jesus bother touching this man? Why didn't he just will him to be healed and get it over with?

What are some different circumstances of life I see that might need to be sanctified? How might I help bring this about?

Heavenly Father, as You created me with senses, help me always to appreciate the unique and irreplaceable encounters with Jesus that the seven sacraments of Your holy Church make available for me and all people. Amen.

JESUS PROCLAIMED THE

GOSPEL *of* THE KINGDOM

AND CURED EVERY DISEASE

AMONG THE PEOPLE.

CF. MATTHEW 4:23

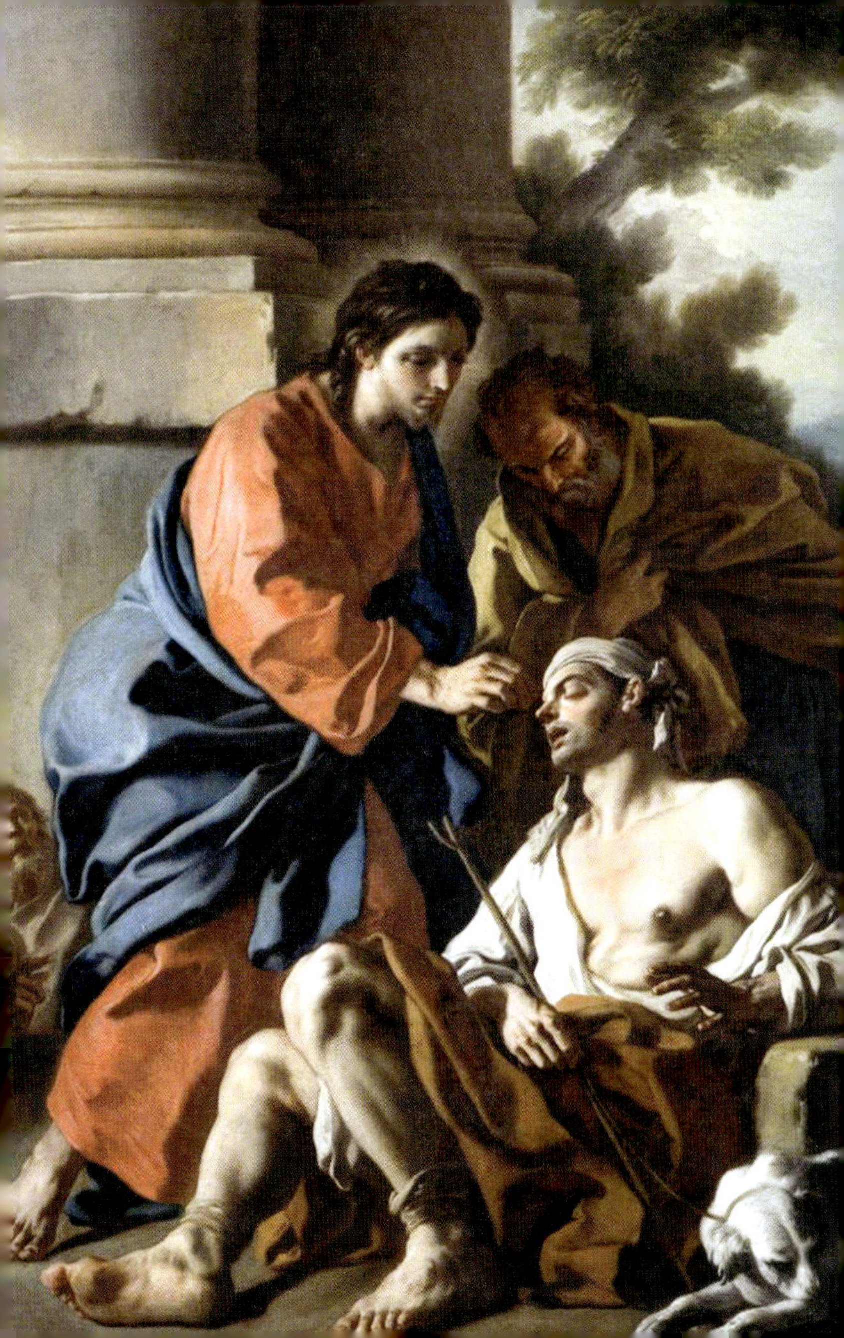

Twenty-Fourth Sunday in Ordinary Time

ISAIAH 50:5–9A

PSALM 116:1–2, 3–4, 5–6, 8–9

JAMES 2:14–18

MARK 8:27–35

Following the Messiah

In today's Gospel, we reach a pivotal moment in our walk with the Lord. After weeks of listening to His words and witnessing His deeds, along with the disciples we're asked to decide who Jesus truly is.

Peter answers for them, and for us, too, when he declares: "You are the Messiah." Many expected the Messiah to be a miracle worker who would vanquish Israel's enemies and restore the kingdom of David (see John 6:15). Jesus today reveals a different portrait. He calls Himself the Son of Man, evoking the royal figure Daniel saw in his heavenly visions (see Daniel 7:13–14). But Jesus' kingship is not to be of this world (see John 18:36). And the path to His throne, as He reveals, is by way of suffering and death.

Jesus identifies the Messiah with the Suffering Servant that Isaiah foretells in today's First Reading. The words of Isaiah's servant are Jesus' words as He gives Himself to be shamed and beaten, trusting that God will be His help. We hear Our Lord's voice again in today's Psalm, as He gives thanks that God has freed Him from the cords of death.

As Jesus tells us today, to believe that He is the Messiah is to follow His way of self-denial—losing our lives to save them, in order to rise with Him to new life. Our faith, we hear again in today's Epistle, must express itself in works of love (see Galatians 5:6).

Notice that Jesus questions the Apostles today "along the way." They are on the way to Jerusalem, where the Lord will lay down His life. We, too, are on a journey with the Lord. We must take up our cross, giving to others and enduring all our trials for His sake and the sake of the Gospel. Our lives must be an offering of thanksgiving for the new life He has given us until that day when we reach our destination and walk before the Lord in the land of the living.

Apparently, human beings (sometimes, at least) think differently than God does. This makes sense because, although we're made in God's image, we are certainly different from God. One significant example is the fact that God is Love, and God is Truth.

> The God of our faith has revealed himself as He who is; and he has made himself known as "abounding in steadfast love and faithfulness" (*Ex* 34:6). God's very being is Truth and Love. (CCC 231)

Denying ourselves might mean turning toward God and toward others. One way we can serve others is by working in the framework of our governmental bodies. When we help embody the gospel of life by working concretely to build a civilization of love, we move toward thinking—and acting—more like God.

It is the duty of citizens to work with civil authority for building up society in a spirit of truth, justice, solidarity, and freedom. (CCC 2255)

MAY I NEVER BOAST EXCEPT IN THE CROSS OF OUR LORD THROUGH WHICH THE WORLD HAS BEEN CRUCIFIED TO ME AND I TO THE WORLD.

GALATIANS 6:14

What in my life might I need to "get behind me"?

In what ways can I work with civil authority to build society in truth, justice, solidarity, and freedom?

Holy Spirit, as You enlightened the Apostles so they acknowledged Jesus as the Messiah, please instruct my heart. Allow me always to know what is right and to constantly enjoy Your holy comforts, through Christ Our Lord. Amen.

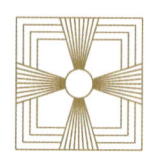

Twenty-Fifth Sunday in Ordinary Time

WISDOM 2:12, 17–20

PSALM 54:3–4, 5, 6 AND 8

JAMES 3:16–4:3

MARK 9:30–37

Servant of All

In today's First Reading, it's like we have our ears pressed to the wall and can hear the murderous grumblings of the elders, chief priests, and scribes—who last week Jesus predicted would torture and kill Him (see Mark 8:31; 10:33–34).

The liturgy invites us to see this passage from the Book of Wisdom as a prophecy of the Lord's Passion. We hear His enemies complain that "the Just One" has challenged their authority. Christ has reproached them for breaking the Law of Moses and betraying their training as leaders and teachers.

And we hear chilling words that foreshadow how they will mock Him as He hangs on the Cross: "For if the Just One be the Son of God, He will . . . deliver Him . . ." (compare Matthew 27:41–43).

Today's Gospel and Psalm give us the flip side of the First Reading. In both, we hear of Jesus' sufferings from His point of view. Though His enemies surround Him, He offers Himself freely in sacrifice, trusting that God will sustain Him.

But the Apostles today don't understand this second announcement of Christ's Passion. They begin arguing over issues of succession, over who among them is greatest, who will be chosen to lead after Christ is killed. Again they are thinking not as God but as human beings (see Mark 8:33). And again Jesus teaches the Twelve—the chosen leaders of His Church—that they must lead by imitating His example of love and self-sacrifice. They must be "servants of all," especially the weak and the helpless, symbolized by the child He embraces and places in their midst.

This is a lesson for us as well. We must have the mind of Christ, who humbled Himself to come among us (see Philippians 2: 5–11). We must freely offer ourselves, making everything we do a sacrifice in praise of His name. As James says in today's Epistle, we must seek wisdom from above, desiring humility not glory, and in all things be gentle and full of mercy.

Children are the supreme gifts of married life. Jesus in this Gospel passage allows a child to help Him make a point. His affection for the child (He didn't have to put His arms around the kid) seems obvious. Jesus seems to think that children are gifts from the One who sent Him.

> Unity, indissolubility, and openness to fertility are essential to marriage. Polygamy is incompatible with the unity of marriage; divorce separates what God has joined together; the refusal of fertility turns married life away from its "supreme gift," the child (GS 50 § 1). (CCC 1664)

The idea of receiving a child can of course be taken several different, complementary ways. Parents are not required to seek large quantities of children for their families in all cases; the number of children that God calls a married couple to accept varies from family to family. What doesn't vary, though, is the moral acceptability of methods for spacing children in a marriage. Some methods, for legitimate intentions, are appropriate—most specifically Natural Family Planning.

NFP is to be distinguished from the old "rhythm method" for which some mistake it even today. Please contact your diocesan offices for accurate, up-to-date information on Natural Family Planning.

> The regulation of births represents one of the aspects of responsible fatherhood and motherhood. Legitimate intentions on the part of the spouses do not justify recourse to morally unacceptable means (for example, direct sterilization or contraception).
> (CCC 2399)

GOD HAS CALLED US THROUGH THE GOSPEL TO POSSESS THE GLORY OF OUR LORD JESUS CHRIST.

CF. 2 THESSALONIANS 2:14

How responsible of a parent am I, either literally (my own children), figuratively (young people in general), or both?

How kid-friendly and family-friendly is my community? How are families with an above-average number of children (in America, a whopping three!) treated? What might I do to help make all of my communities more family- and child-friendly?

Most Blessed Virgin Mary, as Jesus embraces the child in today's Gospel account, please pray that all married couples will be open to new life, imitating Our Lord's example of love and self-sacrifice in nurturing the vocation of each child sent by God. Amen.

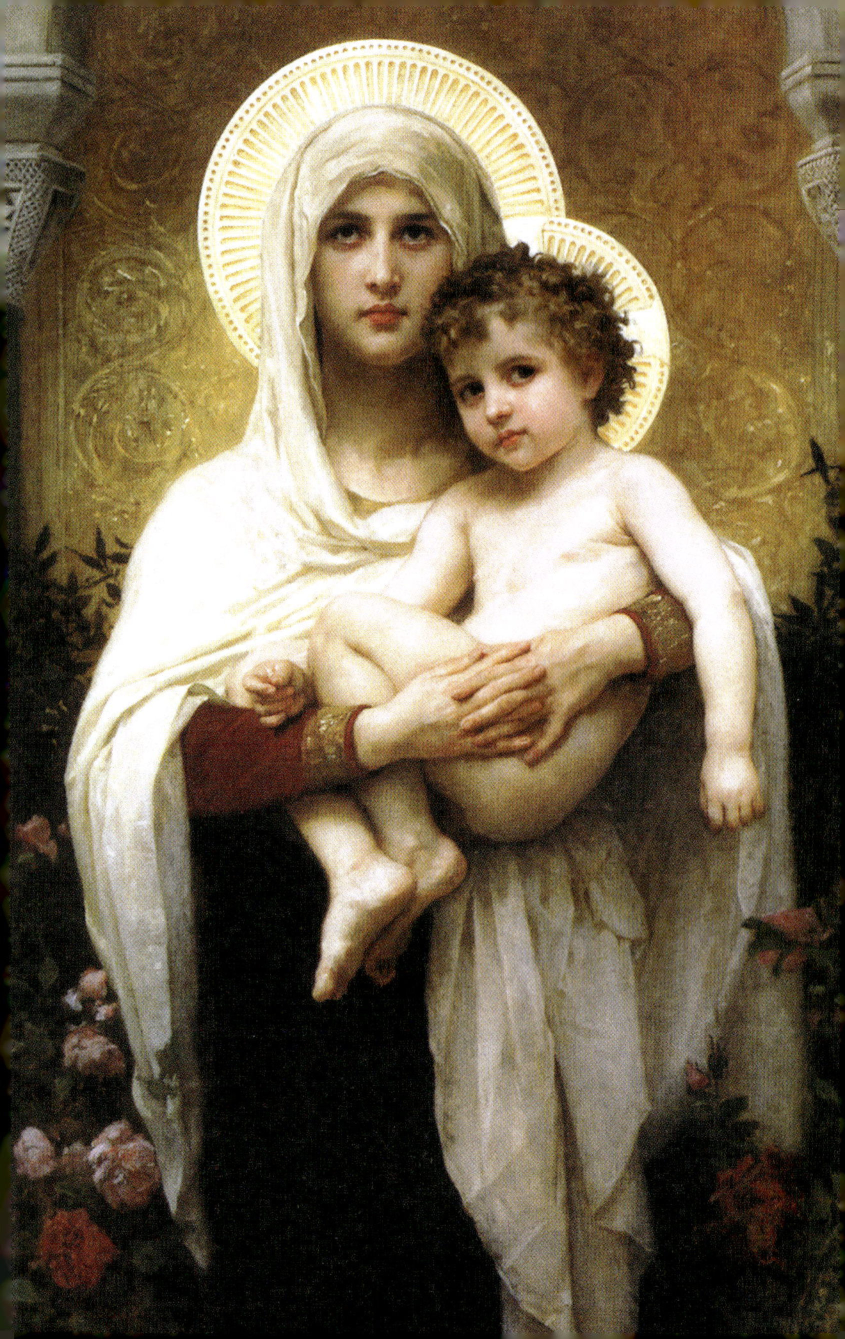

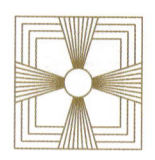

Twenty-Sixth Sunday in Ordinary Time

NUMBERS 11:25–29

PSALM 19:8, 10, 12–13, 14

JAMES 5:1–6

MARK 9:38–43, 45, 47–48

To Belong to Christ

Today's Gospel begins with a scene that recalls a similar moment in the history of Israel, the episode recounted in today's First Reading. The seventy elders who receive God's Spirit through Moses prefigure the ministry of the Apostles.

Like Joshua in the First Reading, John makes the mistake of presuming that only a select few are inspired and entrusted to carry out God's plans. The Spirit blows where it wills (see John 3:8), and God desires to bestow His Spirit on all the people of God in every nation under heaven (see Acts 2:5, 38).

God can and will work mighty deeds through the most unexpected and unlikely people. All of us are called to perform even our most humble tasks, such as giving a cup of water, for the sake of His name and the cause of His kingdom.

John believes he is protecting the purity of the Lord's name. But really, he's only guarding his own privilege and status. It's telling that the Apostles want to shut down the ministry of an exorcist. Authority to drive out demons and unclean spirits was one of the specific powers entrusted to the Twelve (see Mark 3:14–15; 6:7, 13).

"Cleanse me from my unknown faults," we pray in today's Psalm. Often, like Joshua and John, perhaps without noticing it, we cloak our failings and fears under the guise of our desire to defend Christ or the Church. But as Jesus says today, instead of worrying about who is a real Christian and who is not, we should make sure that we ourselves are leading lives worthy of our calling as disciples (see Ephesians 1:4).

Does the advice we give, or the example of our actions, give scandal—causing others to doubt or lose faith? Do we do what we do with mixed motives instead of seeking only the Father's will? Are we living, as this Sunday's Epistle warns, for our own luxury and pleasure and neglecting our neighbors?

We need to keep meditating on His law, as we sing in today's Psalm. We need to pray for the grace to detect our failings and to overcome them.

Whoever is not against us is for us. Many Christians, through no substantial fault of their own, do not live in full communion with the fullness of Christ's Body on earth, the faithful of our Catholic Church. Yet, these Christians share many beliefs and life-giving practices with us; they should be considered sisters and brothers in Jesus, moving, we hope, ever closer to the full unity willed by Our Father.

> Those "who believe in Christ and have been properly baptized are put in a certain, although imperfect, communion with the Catholic Church." (CCC 838, quoting *UR* 3)

Self-control, modesty, purity, chastity. All of us are called to cultivate these dispositions of the heart and live them out to the best of our ability—all by God's grace and mercy. Those who pursue lives of virtue as disciples of Jesus in communion with His holy Church surely will not lose their reward.

> Purity of heart requires the modesty which is patience, decency, and discretion. Modesty protects the intimate center of the person. (CCC 2533)

YOUR WORD, O LORD, IS TRUTH; CONSECRATE US IN THE TRUTH.
CF. JOHN 17:17B, 17A

Who in my life, if anyone, may lead me toward sin? How might I alter this relationship toward the good?

How might I move toward praying in a more focused way for real, honest unity between all who believe in Christ and have been properly baptized?

St. John, as you wrote about Jesus' prayer that all of His disciples would remain united, please pray for authentic unity among all who claim the name of Christian, that we may all be made one by the life-giving, truth-proclaiming power of the Holy Spirit. Amen.

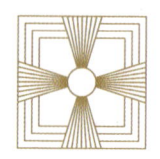

Twenty-Seventh Sunday in Ordinary Time

GENESIS 2:18–24

PSALM 128:1–2, 3, 4–5, 6

HEBREWS 2:9–11

MARK 10:2–16 (OR 10:2–12)

What God Has Joined

In today's Gospel, the Pharisees try to trap Jesus with a trick question. The "lawfulness" of divorce in Israel was never at issue. Moses had long ago allowed it (see Deuteronomy 24:1–4). But Jesus points His enemies back before Moses, to "the beginning," interpreting the text we hear in today's First Reading.

Divorce violates the order of creation, He says. Moses permitted it only as a concession to the people's "hardness of heart"—their inability to live by God's covenant law. But Jesus comes to fulfill the law, to reveal its true meaning and purpose, and to give people the grace to keep God's commands.

Marriage, He reveals, is a sacrament, a divine, life-giving sign. Through the union of husband and wife, God intended to bestow His blessings on the human family, making it fruitful and multiplying it until it filled the earth (see Genesis 1:28).

That's why today's Gospel moves so easily from a debate about marriage to Jesus' blessing of children. Children are blessings the Father bestows on couples who walk in His ways, as we sing in today's Psalm.

Marriage also is a sign of God's new covenant. As today's Epistle hints, Jesus is the New Adam—made a little lower than the angels, born of a human family (see Romans 5:14; Psalm 8:5–7). The Church is the new Eve, the "woman" born of Christ's pierced side as He hung in the sleep of death on the Cross (see John 19:34; Revelation 12:1–17).

Through the union of Christ and the Church as "one flesh," God's plan for the world is fulfilled (see Ephesians 5:21–32). Eve was "mother of all the living" (see Genesis 3:20). In Baptism, we are made sons and daughters of the Church, children of the Father, heirs of the eternal glory He intended for the human family in the beginning.

The challenge for us is to live as children of the kingdom, growing up ever more faithful in our love and devotion to the ways of Christ and the teachings of His Church.

The partnership of woman and man in marriage is so essential to healthy human communities and society that our Church takes it very, very seriously. From the communion of persons in marriage flows all other levels of unity.

> "God did not create man a solitary being. From the beginning, 'male and female he created them' (*Gen* 1:27). This partnership of man and woman constitutes the first form of communion between persons" (*GS* 12 § 4). (CCC 383)

Yes, divorce is one of those actions that is legal but not necessarily moral. When a woman and man freely choose to enter what they truly understand to be a lifelong, God-authored marriage covenant, they are simply not free to dissolve that covenant at will. Volumes of research document divorce's harm to children as well as adults. While each case is different and competent advice should be sought, the bottom line is that reconciliation rather than divorce is the strong preference revealed by the God who loves us, wishes for our best, and makes the amazing possible with His grace.

> The covenant which spouses have freely entered into entails faithful love. It imposes on them the obligation to keep their marriage indissoluble. (CCC 2397)

IF WE LOVE ONE ANOTHER, GOD REMAINS IN US AND HIS LOVE IS BROUGHT TO PERFECTION IN US.

1 JOHN 4:12

How hard is my heart when it comes to accepting specific moral teachings (for example, Jesus' teaching on divorce)?

The Church encourages spouses to seek reconciliation rather than divorce (except in grave situations—and even then, what occurs is essentially a separation rather than immediate pursuit of a divorce per se). If I know any troubled couples, how might I help guide them up the path of reconciliation rather than down divorce's dark road?

Jesus, Mary, and Joseph—Holy Family of Nazareth—please pray that discernment, preparation, and sacramental grace will help all marriages to be happy, healthy, and holy. Amen.

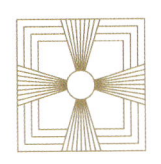

Twenty-Eighth Sunday in Ordinary Time

WISDOM 7:7–11

PSALM 90:12–13, 14–15, 16–17

HEBREWS 4:12–13

MARK 10:17–30 (OR 10:17–27)

Wisdom and Riches

The rich young man in today's Gospel wanted to know what we all want to know: how to live in this life so that we might live forever in the world to come. He sought what today's Psalm calls "wisdom of heart."

He learns that the wisdom he seeks is not a program of works to be performed or behaviors to be avoided. As Jesus tells him, observing the commandments is essential to walking the path of salvation—but it can only get us so far.

The Wisdom of God is not precepts but a person. Jesus is the Wisdom whose Spirit was granted to Solomon in today's First Reading. Jesus is the Word of God spoken of in today's Epistle. And Jesus, as He reveals Himself to the rich man today, is God.

In Jesus we encounter Wisdom, the living and effective Word of God. As He does with the rich man today, He looks upon each of us with love. That loving gaze is a personal invitation to give up everything to follow Him.

Nothing is concealed from His gaze, as we hear in the Epistle. In His fiery eyes the thoughts of our hearts are exposed, and each of us must render an account of our lives (see Revelation 1:14).

We must have the attitude of Solomon, preferring Wisdom to all else, loving Him more than even life itself. This preference, this love, requires a leap of faith. We will be persecuted for this faith, Jesus tells His disciples today. But we must trust in His promise that all good things will come to us in His company.

What, then, are the "many possessions" that keep us from giving ourselves totally to God? What are we clinging to—material things, comfort zones, relationships? What will it take for us to live fully for Christ's sake and the sake of the Gospel? Let us pray for the wisdom to enter into the kingdom of God. With the Psalmist let us ask Him to "Teach us . . . that we may gain wisdom of heart."

"You know the commandments." Essentially, this statement applies to just about everyone. The Ten Commandments aren't some shrouded-in-mystery cryptic code. They are, for the most part, the logical conclusions of God-given human reason left to function unencumbered by self-serving excuses to behave badly. We know the Commandments because God has planted them in our heart and shed further light on them by His revealed truth.

> The Decalogue contains a privileged expression of the natural law. It is made known to us by divine revelation and by human reason. (CCC 2080)

Having many possessions is not bad in and of itself. Getting our priorities mixed up regarding our possessions, though, is an age-old pitfall. Relying on God, focusing on His kingdom over and above acquiring material possessions, will help us use whatever wealth we have wisely, thereby keeping ourselves healthy spiritually as well as physically.

> The goods of creation are destined for the entire human race. The right to private property does not abolish the universal destination of goods. (CCC 2452)

When I consider that all things are possible for God, what challenge in my life might I feel more confident about overcoming?

How well do I make use of my private property in light of the truth that the goods of creation are destined for the entire human race?

Heavenly Father, You gift all people with the natural law so that we might know the basics of how to treat our neighbor. Help me always to acknowledge the wisdom of Your Commandments, striving to live them out by Your grace and mercy. Amen.

BLESSED ARE THE

POOR IN SPIRIT,

for THEIRS IS THE

KINGDOM OF HEAVEN.

MATTHEW 5:3

Twenty-Ninth Sunday in Ordinary Time

ISAIAH 53:10–11

PSALM 33:4–5, 18–19, 20, 22

HEBREWS 4:14–16

MARK 10:35–45 (OR 10:42–45)

Cup of Salvation

The sons of Zebedee hardly know what they're asking in today's Gospel. They are thinking in terms of how the Gentiles rule, of royal privileges and honors. But the road to Christ's kingdom is by way of His Cross. To share in His glory, we must be willing to drink the cup that He drinks.

The cup is an Old Testament image for God's judgment. The wicked would be made to drink this cup in punishment for their sins (see Psalm 75:8; Jeremiah 25:15, 28; Isaiah 51:17). But Jesus has come to drink this cup on behalf of all humanity. He has come to be baptized—which means plunged or immersed—into the sufferings we all deserve for our sins (compare Luke 12:50).

In this He will fulfill the task of Isaiah's Suffering Servant, whom we read about in today's First Reading. Like Isaiah's servant, the Son of Man will give His life as an offering for sin, as once Israel's priests offered sacrifices for the sins of the people (see Leviticus 5:17–19).

Jesus is the heavenly high priest of all humanity, as we hear in today's Epistle. Israel's high priests offered the blood of goats and calves in the temple sanctuary. But Jesus entered the heavenly sanctuary with His own blood (see Hebrews 9:12). And by bearing our guilt and offering His life to do the will of God, Jesus ransomed "the many," paying the price to redeem humanity from spiritual slavery to sin and death.

He has delivered us from death, as we rejoice in today's Psalm.

We need to hold fast to our confession of faith, as today's Epistle exhorts us. We must look upon our trials and sufferings as our portion of the cup He promised to those who believe in Him (see Colossians 1:24).

We must remember that we have been baptized into His Passion and death (see Romans 6:3). In confidence, let us approach the altar today, the throne of grace, at which we drink the cup of His saving blood (see Mark 14:23–24).

How the Twelve understand power is very important to Jesus. He intends to give them authority unparalleled in human history. How will they use it? To serve—even if occasionally this requires tough love? Or to lord it over those entrusted to their care? Thankfully, in the successors of the Twelve, our bishops, we see for the most part power being used in loving service.

> To proclaim the faith and to plant his reign, Christ sends his apostles and their successors. He gives them a share in his own mission. From him they receive the power to act in his person. (CCC 935)

God's preferred way of making authority felt is to help as many people as feasible develop their God-given human potentials—physical, mental, spiritual, emotional, etc. When the goals of those in authority are truly good, pursuing these ends will consist exclusively of using morally suitable methods.

> Authority is exercised legitimately if it is committed to the common good of society. To attain this it must employ morally acceptable means. (CCC 1921)

THE SON OF MAN CAME TO SERVE AND TO GIVE HIS LIFE AS A RANSOM FOR MANY.

MARK 10:45

Power is for service. To what degree do I live up to this teaching?

Do I like to have or wish to have a place of honor at social gatherings? Or am I content not to be the center of attention, to serve as well as being served?

St. John Vianney, patron of parish priests, please pray that all priests will joyfully and effectively serve God's people. Pray also, please, that I will allow the priests in my life to help me grow as a loving, faithful disciple of Jesus. Amen.

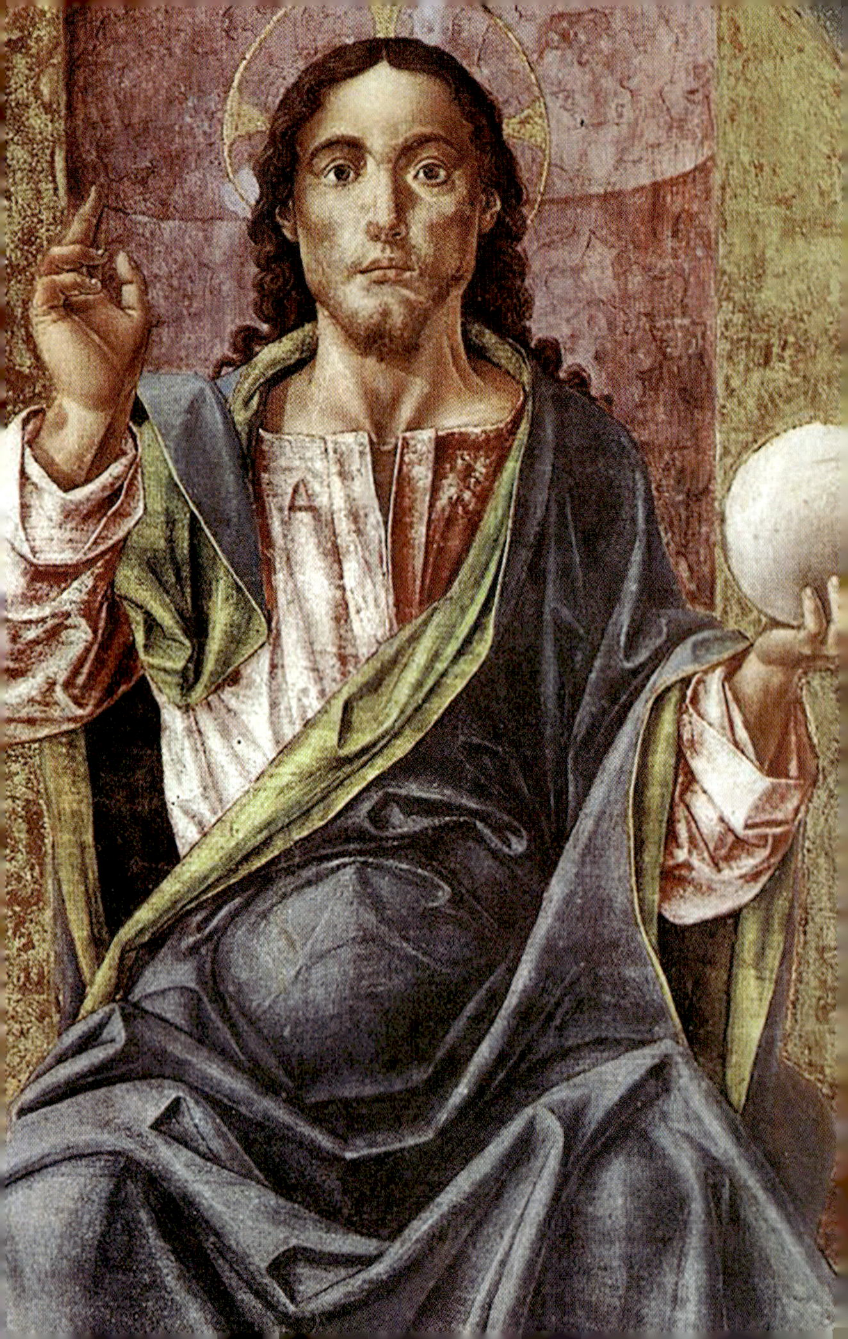

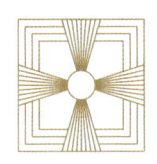

Thirtieth Sunday in Ordinary Time

JEREMIAH 31:7–9

PSALM 126:1–2, 2–3, 4–5, 6

HEBREWS 5:1–6

MARK 10:46–52

Seeing the Son of David

Today's Gospel turns on an irony. It is a blind man, Bartimaeus, who becomes the first after the Apostles to recognize Jesus as the Messiah. And his healing is the last miracle Jesus performs before entering the holy city of Jerusalem for His last week on earth.

The scene on the road to Jerusalem evokes the joyful procession prophesied by Jeremiah in today's First Reading. In Jesus this prophecy is fulfilled. God, through the Messiah, is delivering His people from exile, bringing them back from the ends of the earth, with the blind and lame in their midst.

Jesus, as Bartimaeus proclaims, is the long-awaited Son promised to David (see 2 Samuel 7:12–16; Isaiah 11:9; Jeremiah 23:5). Upon His triumphal arrival in Jerusalem, all will see that the everlasting kingdom of David has come (see Mark 11:9–10).

As we hear in today's Epistle, the Son of David was expected to be the Son of God (see Psalm 2:7). He was to be a priest-king like Melchizedek (see Psalm 110:4), who offered bread and wine to God Most High at the dawn of salvation history (see Genesis 14:18–20).

Bartimaeus is a symbol of his people, the captive Zion of whom we sing in today's Psalm. His God has done great things for him. All his life has been sown in tears and weeping. Now, he reaps a new life. Bartimaeus should also be a sign for us. How often Christ passes us by—in the person of the poor, in the distressing guise of a troublesome family member or a burdensome associate—and yet we don't see Him (see Matthew 25:31–46).

As Jesus sent His Apostles to call Bartimaeus, Christ still calls to us through His Church. Yet, how often are we found to be listening instead to the voices of the crowd, not hearing the words of His Church?

Today He asks us what He asks Bartimaeus, "What do you want me to do for you?" Rejoicing, let us ask the same thing of Him: what can we do in return for all that He has done for us?

Why was Bartimaeus blind? Maybe it was an accident. Maybe someone's sinful, violent act caused his blindness. These would be easy to understand. But what if he was born blind for no apparent reason? Why does God permit physical evil like illness and earthquakes?

First off, the vast majority of evil in our world traces itself back to at least one person's poor choice or decision. As for physical evil—we really don't know, for now, why certain things occur. Yet, we know that ultimately all evil, moral and physical, will be defeated because of Jesus' Passion, death, and Resurrection.

> The fact that God permits physical and even moral evil is a mystery that God illuminates by his Son Jesus Christ who died and rose to

> vanquish evil. Faith gives us the certainty that God would not permit an evil if he did not cause a good to come from that very evil, by ways that we shall fully know only in eternal life. (CCC 324)

Why did Bartimaeus ask for his sight back? Wouldn't a truly admirable person have asked for something less self-centered? This blind man knew that he hadn't earned any favors from Jesus. He needed pity. He sensed, amidst all his needs, that being able to see is a good thing, and asking the Lord of life to restore his sight was okay to do. Jesus, who gives eternal life, freely gave our blind beggar the ability to see. Bartimaeus had faith. He was given a physical good. And he was saved.

> No one can merit the initial grace which is at the origin of conversion. Moved by the Holy Spirit, we can merit for ourselves and for others all the graces needed to attain eternal life, as well as necessary temporal goods. (CCC 2027)

OUR SAVIOR JESUS CHRIST DESTROYED DEATH AND BROUGHT LIFE TO LIGHT THROUGH THE GOSPEL.

2 TIMOTHY 1:10

When physical evil occurs, how do I react? How does my reaction reflect a faith in Jesus Christ?

Do I rebuke people who make their needs known? Do I provide encouragement? How might I help others have their spiritual and material needs satisfied?

Holy Spirit, as You move Your people to seek Jesus, turning away from sin and drawing closer to God, please guide my ongoing conversion, renewing my sense of discipleship each day until this earthly journey ends with eternal life in heaven. Amen.

Thirty-First Sunday in Ordinary Time

DEUTERONOMY 6:2–6

PSALM 18:2–3, 3–4, 47, 51

HEBREWS 7:23–28

MARK 12:28B–34

The Law of Love

Love is the only law we are to live by. And love is the fulfillment of the law that God reveals through Moses in today's First Reading (see Romans 13:8–10; Matthew 5:43–48).

The unity of God—the truth that He is one God, Father, Son, and Spirit—means that we must love Him with one love, a love that serves Him with all our hearts and minds, souls and strength. We love Him because He has loved us first. We love our neighbor because we can't love the God we haven't seen unless we love those made in His image and likeness, whom we have seen (see 1 John 4:19–21).

We are called to imitate the love that Christ showed us in laying His life down on the Cross (see 1 John 3:16). As we hear in today's Epistle, by His perfect sacrifice on the Cross He once and for all makes it possible for us to approach God.

There is no greater love than to lay down your life (see John 15:13). This is perhaps why Jesus tells the scribe in today's Gospel that he is not far from the kingdom of God. The scribe recognizes that the burnt offerings and sacrifices of the Old Law were meant to teach Israel that it is love that He desires (see Hosea 6:6). The animals offered in sacrifice were symbols of the self-sacrifice, the total gift of our selves, that God truly desires.

The readings today should invite us to examine our hearts. Do we have other loves that get in the way of our love for God? Do we love others as Jesus has loved us (see John

13:34–35)? Do we love our enemies and pray for those who oppose and persecute us (see Matthew 5:44)?

Let us tell the Lord we love Him, as we do in today's Psalm. And let us take His Word to heart, that we might prosper and have life eternal in His kingdom, the heavenly homeland flowing with milk and honey.

This scribe, we might presume, heard Jesus proclaim the Good News of salvation from sin and death. Already, though, he seems on the way to forming his conscience excellently, allowing God's grace to penetrate his heart. While God has revealed to us the ordinary way to salvation (and we should pursue it!), God Himself is not limited to this way. God knows a sincere heart when He sees one.

> Those who, through no fault of their own, do not know the Gospel of Christ or his Church, but who nevertheless seek God with a sincere heart, and, moved by grace, try in their actions to do his will as they know it through the dictates of their conscience—those too may achieve eternal salvation. (CCC 847)

To love God as described in this passage sounds like a lot of work. Showing love for our neighbor is of course one way

The Widows' Faith

We must live by the obedience of faith, a faith that shows itself in works of charity and self-giving (see Galatians 5:6). That's the lesson of the two widows in today's liturgy.

The widow in the First Reading isn't even a Jew; yet, she trusts in the word of Elijah and the promise of his Lord. Facing sure starvation, she gives all that she has, her last bit of food, feeding the man of God before herself and her family. The widow in the Gospel also gives all that she has, offering her last bit of money to support the work of God's priests in the temple.

In their self-sacrifice, these widows embody the love that Jesus revealed as the heart of the law and the Gospel in last week's Gospel. They mirror the Father's love in giving His only Son, and Christ's love in sacrificing Himself on the Cross.

Again in today's Epistle we hear Christ described as a new high priest and the Suffering Servant foretold by Isaiah. On the Cross, He made a sacrifice once and for all to take away our sin and bring us to salvation (see Isaiah 53:12).

And again we are called to imitate His sacrifice of love in our own lives. We will be judged not by how much we give—for the scribes and wealthy contribute far more than the widow. Rather, we will be judged by whether our gifts reflect our livelihood, our whole beings, all our heart and soul, mind and strength. Are we giving all that we can to the Lord? And are we giving what we can not out of a sense of forced duty but in a spirit of generosity and love (see 2 Corinthians 9:6–7)?

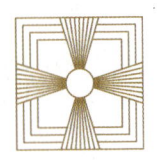

Thirty-Second Sunday in Ordinary Time

1 KINGS 17:10–16

PSALM 146:7, 8–9, 9–10

HEBREWS 9:24–28

MARK 12:38–44 (OR 12:41–44)

WHOEVER LOVES ME
WILL KEEP MY WORD,
SAYS *the* LORD;
AND MY FATHER
WILL LOVE HIM AND
WE WILL COME TO HIM.

JOHN 14:23

to show this love. Another—burnt offerings and sacrifices aside—is participating in liturgical worship. At liturgy we join Jesus, the Head of the Body of Christ, in offering love to Our Father with heart, soul, mind, and strength.

> The liturgy is the work of the whole Christ, head and body. Our high priest celebrates it unceasingly in the heavenly liturgy, with the holy Mother of God, the apostles, all the saints, and the multitude of those who have already entered the kingdom. (CCC 1187)

A person can, through no fault of her or his own, not know the Gospel of Jesus or His Church. But I can be at fault in such cases. How might I avoid being guilty of contributing to ignorance of the Good News?

Jesus gives a compliment to the scribe in this passage. Who in my community needs to hear a compliment from me this week?

All-loving God, love is often misunderstood and mistaken for stances like permissiveness. Please help me to perceive love accurately, express it appropriately, and share it generously in imitation of Jesus. Amen.

The name of the Lord, the Lord Himself, and His Good News of salvation from sin and death all deserve our most profound appreciation and respect.

> The second commandment enjoins respect for the Lord's name. The name of the Lord is holy. (CCC 2161)

BE VIGILANT AT ALL TIMES AND PRAY THAT YOU MAY HAVE THE STRENGTH TO STAND BEFORE THE SON OF MAN.

LUKE 21:36

In what ways do I use the Lord's name? How do these uses reflect a belief that my Lord's name is sacred?

How might I help instill a greater respect for the name of God in my communities?

Heavenly Father, may the hope of my resurrection sustain me in times of tribulation, and may confidence in Your promises help me always to persevere in faith. Amen.

promises to save "the elect," the faithful remnant (see Isaiah 43:6; Jeremiah 32:37).

As today's First Reading tells us, this salvation will include the bodily resurrection of those who sleep in the dust.

We are to watch for this day, when His enemies are finally made His footstool, as today's Epistle envisions. We can wait in confidence knowing, as we pray in today's Psalm, that we will one day delight at His right hand forever.

Jesus said many things to His disciples. Not all of what He said got written down. How did the Gospel writers know what to record and what to let pass? Simply put, God helped them make decisions along these lines. We call this inspiration, and because God was involved in the writing process we can say in a sense that He is an author.

> God is the author of Sacred Scripture because he inspired its human authors; he acts in them and by means of them. He thus gives assurance that their writings teach without error his saving truth (cf. *DV* 11). (CCC 136)

By saying "The Gospel of the Lord," we acknowledge that the Good News is to be held in very high esteem. Why? Because the Lord is holy. All that is associated with His name is holy.

Hope in Tribulation

In this, the second-to-last week of the Church year, Jesus has finally made it to Jerusalem. Near to His Passion and death, He gives us a teaching of hope, telling us how it will be when He returns again in glory.

Today's Gospel is taken from the end of a long discourse in which Jesus describes tribulations the likes of which haven't been seen "since the beginning of God's creation" (see Mark 13:19). He describes what amounts to a dissolution of God's creation, a "devolution" of the world to its original state of formlessness and void.

First, human community—nations and kingdoms—will break down (see Mark 13:7–8). Then, the earth will stop yielding food and begin to shake apart (13:8). Next, the family will be torn apart from within and the last faithful individuals will be persecuted (13:9–13). Finally, the temple will be desecrated and the earth emptied of God's presence (13:14).

In short, God is describing putting out the lights that He established in the sky in the very beginning—the sun, the moon, and the stars (see also Isaiah 13:10; 34:4). Into this "uncreated" darkness, the Son of Man, in whom all things were made, will come.

Jesus has already told us that the Son of Man must be humiliated and killed (see Mark 8:31). Here He describes His ultimate victory, using royal-divine images drawn from the Old Testament: clouds, glory, and angels (see Daniel 7:13). He shows Himself to be the fulfillment of all God's

Thirty-Third Sunday in Ordinary Time

DANIEL 12:1–3

PSALM 16:5, 8, 9–10, 11

HEBREWS 10:11–14, 18

MARK 13:24–32

Endowed with a spiritual soul, with intellect and with free will, the human person is from his very conception ordered to God and destined for eternal beatitude. He pursues his perfection in "seeking and loving what is true and good" (GS 15 § 2). (CCC 1711)

BLESSED ARE THE POOR IN SPIRIT, FOR THEIRS IS THE KINGDOM OF HEAVEN
MATTHEW 5:3

Would I die for the faith? If not literally, how might God be calling me to die for the faith even today?

When I pause to consider that each person in all of my communities is endowed with a spiritual soul, ordered to God and destined for eternal beatitude, what thoughts and feelings does this bring about?

St. John the Baptist, as your zeal for souls motivated you to do what God asked of you, please pray that I'll always love God with all my heart, mind, soul, and strength while generously loving my neighbor as myself. Amen.

Do not be afraid, the man of God tells us today. As we sing in today's Psalm, the Lord will provide for us, as he sustains the widow. Let us follow the widows' example, doing what God asks, confident that our jars of flour will not grow empty nor our jugs of oil run dry.

The poor widow probably never heard of Christ's Church. She may not even have been baptized, even by John. Yet clearly she loves God and is trying sincerely to please Him. God has revealed the ordinary way to salvation because He loves us and wants all to be saved. In extraordinary situations, though, God may save by ways other than Baptism. (Of course He may; He's God, after all!)

> Those who die for the faith, those who are catechumens, and all those who, without knowing of the Church but acting under the inspiration of grace, seek God sincerely and strive to fulfill his will, can be saved even if they have not been baptized (cf. *LG* 16). (CCC 1281)

This widow allows her natural orientation toward God to shine through. Every person is so oriented from the womb, through life and livelihood, right up to the tomb.

Index of Images

The Prophet Isaiah by Michelangelo (c. 1511)	p. 15
Cestello Annunciation by Sandro Botticelli (1489–1490)	p. 20
Adoration of the Shepherds by Gerard van Honthorst (1622)	p. 26
Adoration of the Magi by Matthias Stom (c.1633–1639)	p. 39
The Madonna of Humility after Robert Campin (c.1450–1470)	p. 44
The Calling of Saints Peter and Andrew by Caravaggio (1603–1606)	p. 51
Dispute with the Doctors in the Temple by Veronese (c. 1560)	p. 70
St. John the Baptist Preaching in the Wilderness by Anton Raphael Mengs (c.1760)	p. 80
The Temptation of Christ by Juan de Flandes (c.1500/1504)	p. 87
Ecce Homo by Antonio Ciseri (1871)	p. 97
Jesus Entering Jerusalem by Jaroslav	p. 108
The Resurrection by Sebastiano Ricci (c. 1715–1716)	p. 114
Noli Me Tangere by Fra Angelico (c.1450)	p. 121
Supper at Emmaus by Caravaggio (1601)	p. 131
The Incredulity of St. Thomas by Paolo Moranda Cavazzola (1520)	p. 146
Pentecost by Juan Bautista Maíno (1615–1620)	p. 157
The Holy Trinity by Jan Cornelisz Vermeyen (1530–1540)	p. 169

INDEX OF IMAGES

The Fall of the Rebel Angels by Luca Giordano (c. 1666)	p. 183
The Marriage at Cana by Maerten de Vos (c. 1596–1597)	p. 203
Transfiguration by Peter Paul Rubens (1604–1605)	p. 220
Christ the Savior with the Eucharist by Juan de Juanes (c. 1545–1550)	p. 237
Christ Healing the Blind Man by Francesco de Mura (c. 1716–1782)	p. 251
The Madonna of the Roses by William-Adolphe Bouguereau (1903)	p. 261
Christ Enthroned by Bartolomeo Vivarini (1450)	p. 280
The Coronation of the Virgin by Diego Velázquez (1635–1636)	p. 299